GOD'S ARMOR & ARSENAL
THE ARMOR OF GOD FOR KIDS & TEENS

A DYNAMIC ADVENTURE
THROUGH CHARACTER BUIDING
& DICIPLESHIP

Curriculum inspired by the powerful sermons & teachings of Rev. Greg Cooper.

GOD'S ARMOR & ARSENAL
THE ARMOR OF GOD FOR KIDS & TEENS

Our young people are being targeted like never before in history. They are facing challenges & are exposed to more evils than any generation before them. GOD'S ARMOR & ARSENAL is for this specific time in history. With GOD'S ARMOR & ARSENAL, there is no need for our young people to feel scared, anxious or confused. Never again will they feel inadequate or not enough. They will march boldly into each day knowing they belong to God & have the entire Kingdom of Heaven backing them. They are heirs of God, friends of God, kings & queens, mighty warriors & God's Ambassadors! They are more than enough!

Through a dynamic, twelve-week adventure, each young person will discover that they are children of the most high God, loved beyond measure & made beautifully in the likeness of a mighty God. They will realize the power, protection & countless blessings that are available to them through learning & obeying God's word. GOD'S ARMOR & ARSENALwill teach them how to put on the full Armor of God each day & how to effectively & efficiently wield the weapons God has provided for them in their spiritual arsenal. GOD'S ARMOR & ARSENAL will cultivate a love for God's word through demonstrating how the Bible isn't just a set of rules, but the Living Word of God that can be used to bless them & win every spiritual battle so they can occupy every good & wonderful thing God has prepared for them.

...WE WILL TELL THE NEXT GENERATION THE PRAISEWORTHY DEEDS OF THE LORD, HIS POWER, & THE WONDERS HE HAS DONE.

PSALM 78:4

HOW TO USE THIS BOOK

The next twelve weeks are divided into twelve phases based on Ephesians 6:10-20. Each phase is divided into the following easy to use, challenging & exciting elements:

- **BATTLE PREP:** A special element just for you, the leader of young warriors, which will help prepare your heart & mind for each service.

- **WEAPONS ASSIGNMENT:** This is our Bible verse & each new Bible verse that we learn is another weapon added to our arsenal.

- **COMBAT TRAINING:** A powerful message from the Bible that illustrates how spiritual battles are won with God's word.

- **RECONNAISSANCE:** A deeper look inside the message that will initiate engaging conversation & thought.

- **THE OBJECTIVE:** A fun & easy illustration or object lesson that demonstrates the newly assigned weapon.

- **WEAPONS INSPECTION:** This is where we take a closer look at our weapon & learn how to use it in our daily lives. We will also discuss the specific piece of armor Paul was analogizing in Ephesians 6.

- **THE MISSION:** Take home papers that will encourage & challenge young warriors to apply God's word to their daily lives.

Move through the elements above in each weekly phase. Each element is focused on & derived from the newly assigned weapon from God's word. This will allow you to familiarize yourself with your weapon, see it demonstrated in action & learn how to use it effectively.

TABLE OF CONTENTS

STRONG IN
THE LORD

I BELONG
TO GOD

PHASE 1

PHASE 1: STRONG IN THE LORD
I BELONG TO GOD

BATTLE PREP

READ 1 SAMUEL 16:1-13

Not even Samuel would've known who David was if he hadn't listened to God. Nothing in the world said David was a king; he was too young & didn't seem to fit the part. It's a good thing Samuel didn't listen to the world or even to himself to determine who David was. Samuel listened to God.

What if David didn't listen to Samuel & chose to believe his older, mocking brothers instead? Not even David's dad believed in him. Imagine a soldier in the military who would take orders from anyone, even people who weren't in the military. What if his superior officer told him he was a higher rank but somebody outside of the military told him he was a lower rank? Who is the soldier going to believe? The soldier wouldn't listen to a stranger over his commanding officer about rank, status or mission. That would be absurd, but that's how it is when we listen to anyone other than God to tell us who we are.

Good soldiers know their real strength comes from the military unit they belong to. Even the strongest soldier is outmatched on his own without the rest of the military forces backing him. We belong to God & his heavenly army. Our strength comes from belonging to Christ & knowing who we are according to God. God's Holy Spirit lives inside of us making us strong in the Lord! Ephesians 6:10.

WEAPONS ASSIGNMENT

1 SAMUEL 16:7 But the LORD said to Samuel, "Do not consider his appearance or his height, for I have rejected him. The LORD does not look at the things people look at. People look at the outward appearance, but the LORD looks at the heart."

COMBAT TRAINING

TELL THE STORY OF DAVID BEING ANOINTED KING IN 1 SAMUEL 16

David's brothers were strong on the outside, but David's strength was much greater because his heart belonged to God & he was strong in the Lord. God isn't concerned with how everyone else sees our outward appearance; God cares about the way we think & feel about him on the inside. When we love & believe in Jesus & accept Jesus as our Lord & Savior then we have all the strength of God & Heaven to make us strong in the Lord & we don't need to be concerned with what anyone else thinks of us.

PHASE 1: STRONG IN THE LORD
I BELONG TO GOD

RECONNAISSANCE

- David didn't fit in. He had seven older brothers who bullied him & mocked him. God doesn't want us to fit in with the rest of the world. God wants us to stand out & shine bright with love & kindness. What are some ways you don't fit in with other people but fit in with God?

- David obeyed God & his parents. Obeying God is what gives us power & protection. Since David obeyed God with small things, God trusted him with bigger things like being king. When it comes to obeying God, what are some things you need to work on?

- David didn't look like a king on the outside. His brothers appeared more fitting for the role of king. God created us in Heaven & he knows the wonderful person he created us to be & the things he wants us to do. We should never underestimate ourselves or judge ourselves or anyone else because that is the same as underestimating God. Only God can tell you who you are & he says that you are beautiful, wonderful & strong & he loves you more than anything in the world.

- Not even David's father believed in him & David was chosen last to stand before Samuel. This must have hurt David's feelings a lot, but David didn't act up for being left out, he knew he belonged to God & he only listened to God to tell him who he was. King!

PHASE 1: STRONG IN THE LORD
I BELONG TO GOD

THE OBJECTIVE

YOU WILL NEED one can of tuna & a can of cat food that is the same or similar size. Switch the labels on the two cans prior to church.

Hold up the can of tuna that is now labeled cat food & ask if they think you should eat it. Open the can & begin eating it After the excitement dies down, present the cat food can that is labeled tuna & ask if they think you should eat it. Tell them you won't eat it because no matter what the label says, you know it's a can of cat food because you switched its label with the tuna.

WHAT'S THE POINT? We need labels on cans & jars so we know what's inside of them. Could you imagine if anyone from anywhere could change any label on any can at the store to anything without even knowing what the factory put inside of it? You might think you're buying lotion & end up with mustard! It would be crazy!

God is the only one who can tell us who we are. God created us & loves us. The world, other kids, adults & even our family will try to put labels on us that don't belong. They will say things like you're too young, too old, not good enough, not strong enough, too fat, too thin or any number of things, but if God didn't say it then it isn't so.

God labeled David as a king but not even David's own family saw David as a king. If David listened to what his brothers said instead of God, then he never would have become a mighty king. This is why we need to know whose we are & continually tell ourselves, I belong to God!

WEAPONS INSPECTION

1 SAMUEL 16:7 But the LORD said to Samuel, "Do not consider his appearance or his height, for I have rejected him. The LORD does not look at the things people look at. People look at the outward appearance, but the LORD looks at the heart."

STRONG IN THE LORD: A soldier's true strength comes from having the entire military on his side. Our strength comes from God & belonging to him. Could you imagine a high ranking soldier being told by someone who wasn't even in the military that he was a low rank? Do you think the soldier would believe it? A soldier's rank doesn't change because someone outside of the military says so & who you are doesn't change regardless of what anyone else says about you. You belong to God & it only matters what God says about you. If God didn't say it then it isn't true. God made you & everything God does is wonderful. God never makes mistakes. You're amazing & wonderfully made!

PHASE 1: STRONG IN THE LORD
I BELONG TO GOD

THE MISSION

TO COMPLETE YOUR MISSION YOU WILL NEED THE FOLLOWING WEAPON FROM THE BIBLE: 1 SAMUEL 16:7 But the LORD said to Samuel, "Do not consider his appearance or his height, for I have rejected him. The LORD does not look at the things people look at. People look at the outward appearance, but the LORD looks at the heart."

YOUR MISSION: REMOVE THE LABELS! Don't worry about how other people label you. Tell yourself, I belong to God & I will only believe what God says about me.

WATCH FOR TRAPS: There will always be people that will try to convince you that you are something other than what God says you are. The enemy is any feeling or thought that is telling you that you are less than or anything other than who God says you are.

DEFEAT THE ENEMY: Choose to believe only what God says about you & ignore the rest. Remember David & how God said he was a king but not even his own family believed it & labeled him as less. Just like David, your heart belongs to God & the spirit of God lives inside of you & makes you strong in the Lord!

LIST AS MANY THINGS AS YOU CAN THAT YOU LIKE ABOUT YOURSELF:

SPIRITUAL
BATTLE

OBEYING GOD
GIVES ME
POWER &
PROTECTION

PHASE 2

PHASE 2: SPIRITUAL BATTLE
OBEYING GOD GIVES ME POWER & PROTECTION

BATTLE PREP

READ 1 PETER 3:8-22

The Bible is full of Godly people who were hated by the majority & falsely accused. Noah, David, Daniel, Joseph, Elijah & Jesus are just a few who suffered because of their faith..Jesus told us that we would also be treated like this, John 15:18-21. The reason the world doesn't like us is because they don't know Jesus. Just as God uses us to do his work, satan also uses people & they are seldom aware of it. The forces controlling their lives recognize God's Holy Spirit inside of us & satan tries to destroy us through them. We don't have to worry about this though, God didn't leave us powerless. The victory has already been secured for us through Christ. In fact, it's awesome when people come against us while we are being obedient to God. This means the enemy considers us a powerful threat. Not only that, every time we are under attack, it is an opportunity to magnify God so others may come to know him. These are times when we can experience God's miraculous power, protection & blessings. Not only are we able to experience God at work in our lives but people who don't know Jesus are able to witness God's love, kindness, grace, power, protection & blessings at work. Just imagine what would have happened if Noah fought back when he was being mocked & ridiculed. He would have never had time to build the ark. The battle isn't against other people. The Bible tells us it is a spiritual battle, Ephesians 6:12.

WEAPONS ASSIGNMENT

1 PETER 3:9 Do not repay evil with evil or insult with insult. On the contrary, repay evil with blessing, because to this you were called so that you may inherit a blessing.

COMBAT TRAINING

TELL THE STORY OF NOAH & THE ARK IN GENESIS 7-9

The Bible tells us that we are fighting a spiritual battle & that our fight isn't against other people but within ourselves to make the right choice no matter what anyone else says or does. It can be hard to be kind to somebody who is not kind to you, but we need to look at things the way God sees them. When somebody is unkind to us, it is because they don't know the love of Jesus. Being mean back to people who are mean to you can keep you from accomplishing the work God has for you to do & it can also keep that person from coming to know Jesus & this is what satan really wants. If Noah was mean to all the people who were mean to him, he would have never been able to complete his work of building the ark, but Noah loved God & was obedient to God, so God protected Noah & his family & gave him the power to overcome & accomplish what God called him to do.

PHASE 2: SPIRITUAL BATTLE
OBEYING GOD GIVES ME POWER & PROTECTION

RECONNAISSANCE

- Before the flood, everyone on Earth was bad & evil except Noah & his family. Noah didn't do what everyone else did. Noah obeyed God.

- People mocked Noah & laughed at him for building an ark. Noah ignored what people said about him & continued to obey God. What do you think would have happened if Noah argued & fought back with those people?

- Noah wasn't rude or unkind to anyone even when they were mean to him. Noah knew his power & protection came from God, so he was obedient to God & never repaid evil with evil. When people are unkind to us, do you think being unkind back to them will help them to know Jesus?

- Noah focused on obeying God, building the ark & doing the work God wanted him to do. Because Noah obeyed God, he & his family were saved & protected.

- Even though nobody else obeyed God, Noah still chose to do what was right. Obeying God gave Noah power & protection. Did you ever have a time when others were doing something wrong but you chose to do what was right instead?

PHASE 2: SPIRITUAL BATTLE
OBEYING GOD GIVES ME POWER & PROTECTION

THE OBJECTIVE

YOU WILL NEED one cell phone with its protective case & a phone charger. You will also need a charger & protective case that are made for a different type of phone & will not work with or fit the phone.

Hold up the cell phone & the charger that isn't made for the phone & demonstrate how the charger does not fit into the phone then toss it aside. Then try placing the phone into the case that isn't made for it & toss the useless case aside. Ask why you can't just use any charger or protective case you want to power & protect your phone. Finally, place the phone in the case that was made for it & then charge it with the charger that was made for the phone to demonstrate how well it works when you choose to power & protect your phone with the items that were specifically made for it.

WHAT'S THE POINT? For our phones to have power & protection, we must use a charger & case that is specifically made to fit our phones. We wouldn't try to power it with a charger that didn't fit or try to protect it in a case that wasn't made for it. That would be useless. Our phone would be without power & protection. As Christians, we need Godly power to accomplish all the great things God wants us to do & we need God's protection every single day. God's word was made specifically for us & obeying God's word gives us power & protection. People who don't know Jesus will tell us all sorts of things that God never intended for us. They will say things like we're weak if we're kind to people who are not kind to us. They might laugh at us or make fun of us if we aren't mean to people who are being mean to us, but Obeying God's word gives us the power & protection that we need to get through each day & carry out the mission God has for us.

WEAPONS INSPECTION

1 PETER 3:9 Do not repay evil with evil or insult with insult. On the contrary, repay evil with blessing, because to this you were called so that you may inherit a blessing.

SPIRITUAL BATTLE: Good soldiers are on a mission to save & rescue people. Sometimes, to do this, they have to fight the enemy, but they would never attack the people they were sent to help. They know exactly who the enemy is & isn't, & they only fight battles they were commanded to fight. Our battle isn't with other people; our battle is spiritual & we fight it with spiritual weapons. Our battles are won through prayer & by demonstrating God's love for the world through our kindness to others & obedience to God.

PHASE 2: SPIRITUAL BATTLE
OBEYING GOD GIVES ME POWER & PROTECTION

THE MISSION

TO COMPLETE YOUR MISSION YOU WILL NEED THE FOLLOWING WEAPON FROM THE BIBLE: 1 PETER 3:9 Do not repay evil with evil or insult with insult. On the contrary, repay evil with blessing, because to this you were called so that you may inherit a blessing.

YOUR MISSION: KNOW YOUR ENEMY! satan (We don't capitalize satan because with God, satan is too small & unimportant.) is your enemy. satan is on a mission to destroy you, but he can never destroy you when you obey God. When somebody is unkind to you, choose to obey God. Before you react, stop, pray & remind yourself, obeying God gives me power & protection.

WATCH FOR TRAPS: satan will use people who don't know Jesus to try to make you disobey God. There will always be people who say mean things or hurt your feelings in some way. These people need Jesus. Don't allow satan to fool you like he is fooling them. Obey God, be kind & pray for these people so they may come to know Jesus.

DEFEAT THE ENEMY: Every time you obey God, you become stronger & more powerful. Obeying God gives you the power you need to accomplish the many good & exciting things God has for you to do. Keep choosing to be kind when others are not. You can do it! Remember how badly Noah was treated by people that didn't know God. Noah knew if he disobeyed God, he wouldn't have had the power he needed to protect himself & his family & experience the wonderful life God had for him. Noah knew it was a spiritual battle & you know it too! Obeying God & showing the world God's love & kindness gives you power & protection. Keep up the good work, soldier!

TAKE A
STAND

BEING GREAT
IS BEING
DIFFERENT

PHASE 3

PHASE 3: TAKE A STAND
BEING GREAT IS BEING DIFFERENT

BATTLE PREP

READ DANIEL 3
Amazing. Extraordinary. Incredible. Uncommon. Unimaginable. Our God is all that & more & so are his creations & this includes you!

When we think of people who changed the course of history, we may think of people such as Joan of Arc, Abraham Lincoln, Mother Teresa or Martin Luther King Jr. We recognize these people because of the choices & sacrifices they made that changed & touched the lives of so many. If you're reading this right now, God has put you in a position to change the course of history. You have been given one of the most amazing opportunities to increase the Kingdom of Heaven & change the lives of more people than you could ever imagine. You have been entrusted to teach, train & lead young Christian warriors! Because of your willingness & obedience, these young people will have the strength & wisdom they need to go out into the world, take their stand for Christ & win the lost.

You pose a great threat to the enemy & just like every other history maker since the beginning of time, you will have one thing in common with these uncommon people. Adversity. Just remember, the greater the battle is, the greater the victory will be. Don't get discouraged when you feel surrounded by problems & hardships. Don't allow anyone or anything to stop you from doing what you were called to do. Take a stand! Stand with the full armor of God, divinely equipped & fully prepared. Ephesians 6:12.

WEAPONS ASSIGNMENT

ROMANS 12:2 Do not conform to the pattern of this world, but be transformed by the renewing of your mind. Then you will be able to test & approve what God's will is-his good, pleasing & perfect will.

COMBAT TRAINING

TELL THE STORY OF SHADRACH, MESHACH & ABEDNEGO IN DANIEL 3
Shadrach, Meshach & Abednego were great men of God, but being great isn't always easy. Being great means being different from everyone else. The entire kingdom was bowing down but they took a stand. They didn't worry about what others thought of them, they weren't concerned with making friends, they only wanted to please God. To be great, you have to be different by doing what God wants you to do & not whatever everyone else is doing. If you act like everyone else, then you are just ordinary. God made you extraordinary.

PHASE 3: TAKE A STAND
BEING GREAT IS BEING DIFFERENT

RECONNAISSANCE

- Shadrach, Meshach & Abednego were taken as slaves & a lot of their family & friends were killed. Even though bad things happened to them, they didn't turn away from God.

- Shadrach, Meshach & Abednego didn't look like everyone else & they spoke a different language. They worshipped the one true God when everyone else worshipped idols, but they never changed to fit in. They continued to pray & worship God. What are some things that make you different from others?

- Others were jealous of Shadrach, Meshach & Abednego & tried to get them in trouble when they weren't doing anything wrong. However, they were never mean back but helped others & did their best work. How do you respond to unkindness from others?

- When the entire city was bowing down to an idol, Shadrach, Meshach & Abednego chose to stand. They took a stand & chose to be different & because of this they were saved. What are some things others do that you choose not to do because you know it is wrong?

THE OBJECTIVE

YOU WILL NEED a piece of black construction paper cut into ten squares of equal size & one square of the same size cut from another piece of paper that is white, so you have ten black squares & one different square that really stands out.

Place your squares on the table & choose one child to come up & pick one square. If they pick the white square then give them a small prize. If they pick a black square, thank them & have them take their square back to their seat but don't give them a prize. Call upon another child & do this until one of them picks the square that is different & receives a prize for picking the winning square.

WHAT'S THE POINT? All of the squares except for one are the same. There is nothing special about the squares that are all the same, but the different square is special because it's a winner. The winning square stood out. When we act like everyone else in the world & do things that we know are wrong because everyone else is doing them then we blend in & there is nothing great about that. Acting like everyone else might even make more people like us & make us more popular but there isn't anything great about being like everyone else. There is no prize in being the same as everyone else. If we want to be great like God made us to be then we need to be different. We have to take a stand & choose to obey God & his word & be different because being great means being different.

PHASE 3: TAKE A STAND
BEING GREAT IS BEING DIFFERENT

WEAPONS INSPECTION

ROMANS 12:2 Do not conform to the pattern of this world, but be transformed by the renewing of your mind. Then you will be able to test & approve what God's will is-his good, pleasing & perfect will.

TAKE A STAND: When you see an elite soldier, he stands out. Even if he isn't wearing a uniform, there are things that are different about him that make him stand out from ordinary people. He stands tall & sturdy in tip-top shape, organized, prepared & ready for anything. He is also held to different standards than regular citizens. Civilians or people that aren't in the military have to obey the laws. Soldiers have to obey those same laws but they also have another set of instructions that they must obey 24/7, even when they are off duty. There are certain places they aren't allowed to go & certain things they aren't allowed to do that may be legal for everyone else. They have to keep their hair cut a certain way, their body in shape & free from things that pollute it & they have to carry themselves in a respectful manner at all times. This makes them stand out, but it is also what makes them so great. As Christian warriors, we have to not only obey the law but also all of God's instructions in the Bible. Sure, this might make us stand out, but there is nothing great about being like everyone else. Being great is being different.

PHASE 3: TAKE A STAND
BEING GREAT IS BEING DIFFERENT

THE MISSION

TO COMPLETE YOUR MISSION, YOU WILL NEED THE FOLLOWING WEAPON OUT OF THE BIBLE: ROMANS 12:2 Do not conform to the pattern of this world, but be transformed by the renewing of your mind. Then you will be able to test & approve what God's will is-his good, pleasing & perfect will.

YOUR MISSION: TAKE A STAND! Choose to follow Jesus & do what's right even when others around you don't live for God. Don't fit in. Be great!

WATCH FOR TRAPS: Others around you will do wrong & won't think it's a big deal but you can still choose to do what's right. If someone is talking badly about someone else, you can choose to say something kind. That's different! If someone does or says something mean to you, choose to respond with kindness. That's different! Obey your parents even when others don't respect theirs. Remember, you're different & that's what makes you so great!

DEFEAT THE ENEMY: Being great isn't easy, it means being different. Most of the great people in history were different. Great people stand out & often don't have a lot of friends because they are different. Never choose how you will behave & who you will be based on what everyone else in the world is doing, instead choose to be who God created you to be. God created you to be great, so take a stand & be different because you can never be great by being like everyone else. You are not made to be like the world. You're special. You're great!

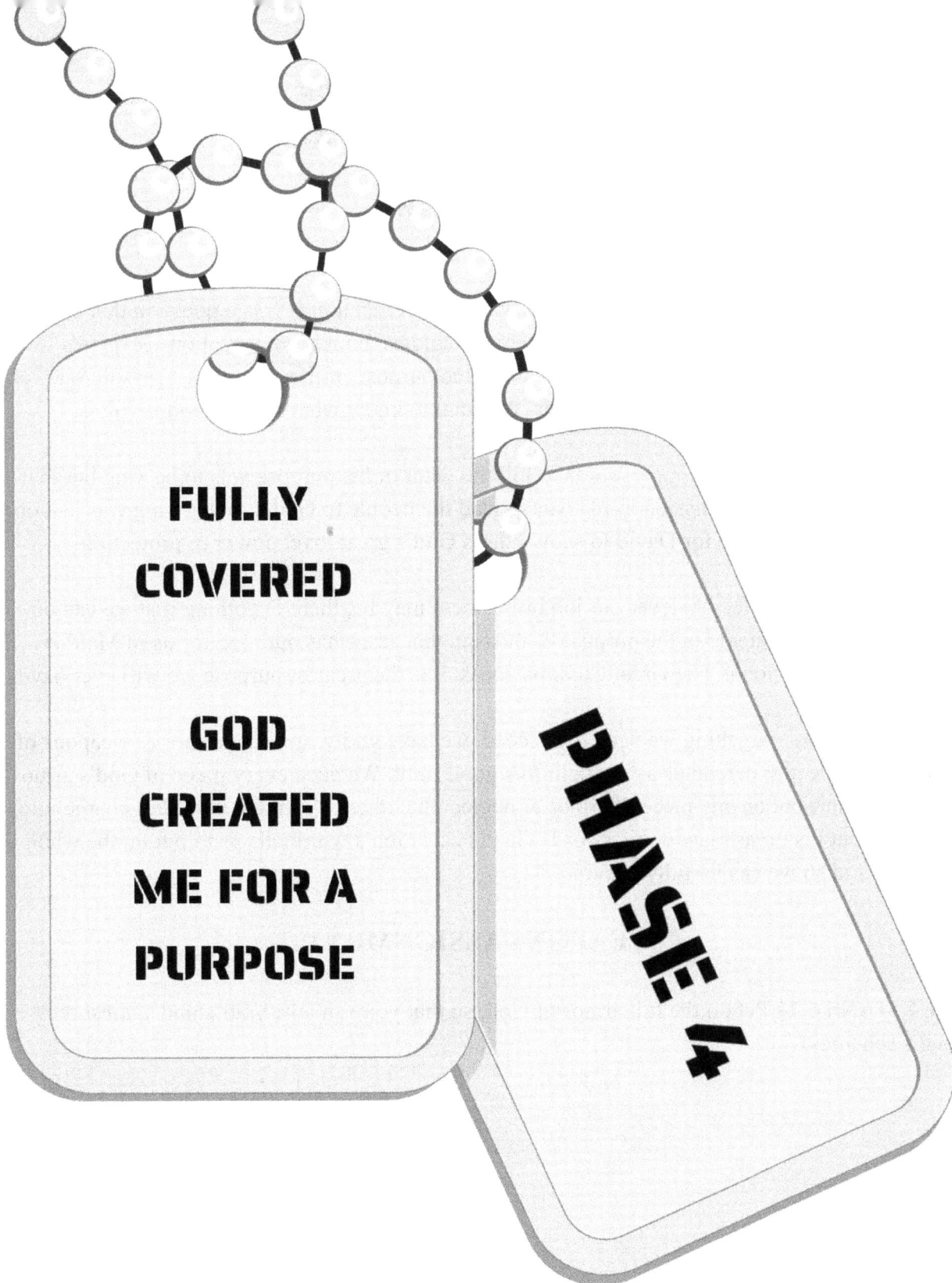

FULLY
COVERED

GOD
CREATED
ME FOR A
PURPOSE

PHASE 4

PHASE 4: FULLY COVERED
GOD CREATED ME FOR A PURPOSE

BATTLE PREP

READ 1 SAMUEL 17
Have you ever wondered what your purpose was? You're not alone. It is a question that everyone asks & wants to know about themselves. There are studies, books, conversations & quotes from people of all walks of life & every religion about the purpose of life. We want a reason & a purpose to exist. We want our life to matter. We want to know what our mission in life is.

Some may say that David's purpose was to kill the giant or his purpose was to be king but that isn't exactly so. David's mission in life was to lead the people to God & being king was just one of the ways God planned for David to show others God's great love, power & protection.

Wherever we are in life, whatever our job or business may be, there is nothing that we can do that will ever be greater than the purpose & mission that Jesus has outlined for us in Matthew 28:18-20. Our mission is The Great Commission & it is the greatest purpose we will ever have.

God has given us everything we need to succeed, we have godly, spiritual armor & weapons of warfare to protect & defend us as we fight this good fight. We need every piece of God's armor daily. You can't put on one piece of armor & neglect the others. A soldier wouldn't charge into battle without his breastplate or his sword. This is why God's word tells us to put on the whole armor of God so we can be fully covered.

WEAPONS ASSIGNMENT

EPHESIANS 6:11 Put on the full armor of God, so that you can take your stand against the devil's schemes.

COMBAT TRAINING

TELL THE STORY OF DAVID & GOLIATH IN 1 SAMUEL 17

Can you imagine a king being told to take out the trash or do the dishes? David was already anointed to be the next king of Israel when he was home tending sheep & doing chores. To make it worse, he had to go to the army camp like a servant girl to give his brothers food. David didn't complain or argue but he stayed focused on his purpose. What do you think would have happened if David disobeyed his parents & refused to take food to his brothers?

David was created for a great purpose & so were you. God has given each & every one of us a mission in life. What do you think David's mission & purpose in life was? It wasn't to kill the giant or become king, it was to lead people to God. Jesus gave all of us that same mission & it is called The Great Commission. Telling others about Jesus & showing the world God's love is The Great Commission. It's our greatest purpose. To complete our mission, we need to be fully covered in God's spiritual armor. David couldn't wear Saul's armor because it didn't fit but he wore God's spiritual armor daily & he was protected, victorious & fully covered.

RECONNAISSANCE

- David was already anointed king when he was told to go take food to his brothers at the army camp. Taking food to soldiers was something women & girls did, not men & certainly not kings but David didn't complain or argue, he did what was required of him. Do you think David would have ever fought Goliath if he disobeyed his parents & refused to go take food to his brothers?

- When David saw a giant tormenting God's people, he wanted to help but his brothers mocked him & accused him of things that weren't true. David didn't argue back but stayed focused on what needed to be done. What do you think would have happened if David argued with his brothers instead of staying focused on the problem with the giant?

- David couldn't wear Saul's armor because it didn't fit him & it was too heavy. Instead, David trusted in God & was fully covered & protected in God's spiritual armor.

PHASE 4: FULLY COVERED
GOD CREATED ME FOR A PURPOSE

THE OBJECTIVE

YOU WILL NEED a glass vase or glass figurine & enough bubble wrap to cover it, a box that is the size you would use to mail your fragile item.

Explain that you need to ship your priceless family heirloom to a family member in another state & you want to make sure it is fully protected. Ask if you should just toss it in the box or use bubble wrap. Next, ask if you should only bubble wrap half of it or all of it. Then ask why they don't think only wrapping half of it will fully protect it. Allow them to express their thoughts.

WHAT'S THE POINT? Just like David was protected with God's spiritual armor when he fought Goliath, God has the same spiritual armor for us & we need every piece of it to be fully covered. We can't just obey some of the Bible & ignore other parts. We need every bit of God's protection to carry out our mission of rescuing the lost for Jesus. The first piece in God's armor is Jesus. Jesus is our belt of truth & without him we have no purpose. Next, we have the breastplate of righteousness, sandals of peace, shield of faith, helmet of salvation & the sword of the spirit, which is the word of God, the Bible. We will learn more about each piece of God's armor in the weeks to come.

Remember your greatest purpose is to lead others to God by showing them the love & kindness of Jesus. Be kind & don't forget to invite a friend to church!

WEAPONS INSPECTION

EPHESIANS 6:11 Put on the full armor of God, so that you can take your stand against the devil's schemes.

FULLY COVERED: Whether a Roman soldier from thousands of years ago or a soldier today, they would never go into battle without being fully covered with all the armor, equipment & protective gear available to them. If a soldier was wearing his helmet but not his breastplate or bullet proof vest, where do you think the enemy is going to aim? The enemy is going to attack the part that isn't covered. As Christians, we face challenges & battles everyday. We are tempted to do things God doesn't want us to do. People aren't always kind & we are tempted to say things that God doesn't want us to say. Sometimes, we don't always feel like doing things that we know we should do, but we choose to do them because we know that's what God wants from us. To be fully covered in God's spiritual armor, we have to choose to obey God every time, all the time. Obeying God is how we complete every mission & purpose God created us for.

PHASE 4: FULLY COVERED
GOD CREATED ME FOR A PURPOSE

THE MISSION

TO COMPLETE YOUR MISSION YOU WILL NEED THE FOLLOWING WEAPON FROM THE BIBLE: EPHESIANS 6:11 Put on the full armor of God, so that you can take your stand against the devil's schemes.

YOUR MISSION: THE GREAT COMMISSION! Tell someone about Jesus this week & invite them to church. Remember to show the world God's love by being kind. The only way others will come to know God & his great love is through our love & kindness. You can do it!

WATCH FOR TRAPS: When you start telling others about Jesus & inviting them to church, there will be people that may make fun of you. Remember David. He didn't let it phase him when his brothers teased & mocked him. He stayed focused & so will you. Keep obeying God & you will be fully covered to complete every purpose God created you for.

DEFEAT THE ENEMY: God loves you more than anything & he made you exactly who you are for a purpose. There are people that you can lead to God that nobody else will be able to reach. God believes in you; he knows how amazing you are because he created you. God has you fully covered for The Great Commission. Be brave. You have more courage than you know. God chose you because he knows you can do it. Show the world God's love & kindness. Ignore anyone trying to distract you from completing your mission. Invite a friend to church so they can learn more about God & his great love for them.

BELT OF
TRUTH

JESUS
IS THE
ONLY WAY

PHASE 5

PHASE 5: BELT OF TRUTH
JESUS IS THE ONLY WAY

BATTLE PREP

READ 1 KINGS 3

What would you ask for if you could be granted anything you wanted? We already have so much to be thankful for so what is it that you need that you don't already have? Solomon was already king when God asked him what he wanted. Solomon already had riches but that has never stopped kings or leaders from wanting more. He could have asked for more territory or any number of things but Solomon put God first & asked for wisdom so he could be a fair, just & godly king.

Since Solomon put God first, God added all the other blessings to him that he could have asked for instead. Jesus is our belt of truth & when we make him the center of our lives then every other piece falls into place according to God's perfect plan. Jesus is the only way to Heaven & the only way we can live a victorious life.

WEAPONS ASSIGNMENT

MATHEW 6:33 But seek first his kingdom & his righteousness, & all these things will be given to you as well.

COMBAT TRAINING

TELL THE STORY OF KING SOLOMON & HIS DREAM IN 1 KINGS 3

Solomon could have asked for anything in the world, but he only wanted the wisdom to lead the way God wanted him to. He could have asked for absolutely anything, but since he put God first, God gave him all the other things as well. When we put Jesus first & make him the Lord of our lives then everything else falls into place. We still have challenges, but we have the ability & the wisdom to face every problem that comes our way. We have all of Heaven backing us & God blessing us. Jesus is the only way to Heaven & the only way we can accomplish all the wonderful things God has prepared for us.

PHASE 5: BELT OF TRUTH
JESUS IS THE ONLY WAY

RECONNAISSANCE

- Before God ever appeared to Solomon in a dream, Solomon was living his life in a way that was pleasing to God. He was already obeying God & doing his best to serve him. If Solomon wasn't living a godly life, he would have never gone to sacrifice to him & God would have never appeared to him in a dream. What are some things you might need to get rid of or stop doing or even start doing more of so you can be closer to God & experience everything God has in store for you?

- When Solomon went to give offerings to God, he was praying & praising & giving thanks to God. Solomon acknowledged God with the way he lived & with his words of praise. What do you think would have happened if Solomon was complaining instead of praising & giving thanks to God?

- When God came to Solomon in a dream & said that he would grant him anything he asked for, Solomon chose to ask for godly wisdom instead of riches or worldly power. Since Solomon put God first, everything else was also given to him & until this day there has been nobody else like him. What would you ask for if God said you could have anything at all? What is it that you want most?

PHASE 5: BELT OF TRUTH
JESUS IS THE ONLY WAY

THE OBJECTIVE

YOU WILL NEED A Jar such as a Mason jar, one large candy bar that is as long as the jar is tall, M&M'S with & without peanuts.

The large candy bar represents God, the peanut M&M'S represent good things that God wants us to do like spending time with family, doing schoolwork & learning new things. The plain M&M's represent things that you like to do for fun like playing games or watching television.

Dump the plain M&M'S into the jar while explaining that they represent the fun stuff that we enjoy, then add the M&M'S with peanuts & explain what they represent. Lastly, demonstrate how the candy bar that represents God does not fit into the jar because we chose to put everything else in our life first & we have no room left for God.

Dump everything out of the jar & stand the candy bar up in the center of the jar, add the peanut M&M'S around the candy bar then pour in the plain M&M'S, showing that everything fits when you place the candy bar in the center before anything else. Make sure to test this out beforehand so you have just the right amount of candies to fill the jar.

WHAT'S THE POINT? If we want to do all the great things God has planned for us to do then we must put Jesus first in our lives. This means taking the time to learn his word, obeying his word, praying & talking to him, praising & thanking him & asking for his help & guidance like King Solomon did. When we put other things first then we don't have time or room for God but when we put God first, he will make a way so that we will be able to do the good things that we enjoy too like spending time with our family & friends & even playing games.

WEAPONS INSPECTION

MATHEW 6:33 But seek first his kingdom & his righteousness, & all these things will be given to you as well.

THE BELT OF TRUTH: The most important piece of the Roman soldiers' armor was his belt. It was the first thing he put on & if it wasn't put on correctly then he would not be able to attach the other parts of his armor or carry his weapons or sword. The belt was the center of his defense & protection. The breastplate attached to his belt, as did the sword & other tools & weapons. Without the belt, he had nothing. One of the most severe punishments given to a Roman soldier was to strip him of his belt because without his belt he was nothing. Jesus is our belt of truth & without him we are powerless. When we make Jesus the center of our life, there is nothing that we cannot do.

PHASE 5: BELT OF TRUTH
JESUS IS THE ONLY WAY

THE MISSION

TO COMPLETE YOUR MISSION YOU WILL NEED THE FOLLOWING WEAPON FROM THE BIBLE: MATHEW 6:33 But seek first his kingdom & his righteousness, & all these things will be given to you as well.

YOUR MISSION: PUT ON YOUR BELT OF TRUTH! You do this by putting God first & making him the center of your life. As soon as you wake up in the morning, say a prayer & thank God for your day & ask him to help you to put him first. Ask God to give you godly wisdom & to show you how to better serve him. Say a prayer & give thanks to God before you eat. Before you play with friends or spend time doing something else you enjoy, take a few moments to memorize your Bible verse & learn God's word. If you know something isn't pleasing to God, then put God first by obeying him & choosing not to do anything that you know isn't good. You can do it even if it is hard at times. Jesus is the only way!

WATCH FOR TRAPS: Putting God first will make you a strong & wise warrior for Jesus. Don't forget to pray first thing when you wake up & praise God & ask for his help. You might need a reminder when you first start doing this. Write yourself a note & put it somewhere that you are sure to see it, like beside your bed or on the mirror. You will have days where things go wrong & it might get tough but instead of complaining, stay positive & focus on everything good in your life & continue to praise God. Remember, it's okay to play games, watch television & do other things you enjoy, but put God first, & don't allow yourself to participate in anything that you feel may be displeasing to God. If at any time you realize that something is wrong, choose to stop it immediately & put God first.

DEFEAT THE ENEMY: Make Jesus the center of your life by choosing to learn more about him & his word, the Bible. Keep memorizing your Bible verses. Pray each morning & at night before you go to bed. Talk to God throughout your day. He loves you & wants you to tell him everything & ask for his help. If you realize something is wrong or you're unsure, then stop whatever it is & choose to do something you know is good instead. Jesus is the only way to Heaven & putting him first is the only way to experience all the great things he has for you in this life. You're doing a great job. You're getting stronger & wiser every day. You've got this!

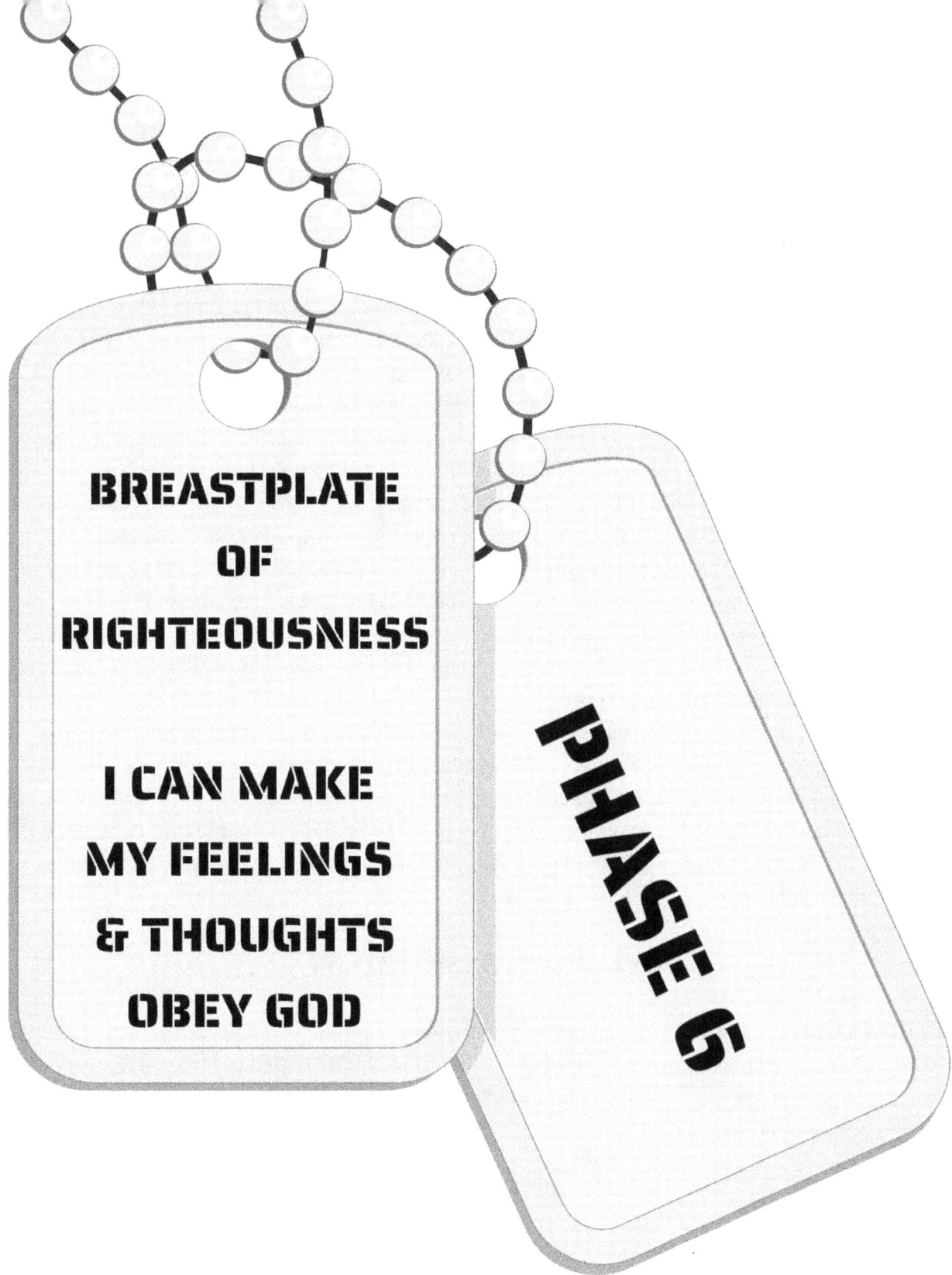

BREASTPLATE
OF
RIGHTEOUSNESS

I CAN MAKE
MY FEELINGS
& THOUGHTS
OBEY GOD

PHASE 6

PHASE 6: BREASTPLATE OF RIGHTEOUSNESS
I CAN MAKE MY FEELINGS & THOUGHTS OBEY GOD

BATTLE PREP

READ ACTS 16

We've all been in situations where things just don't go our way. There are times when, regardless of what we do or how much effort we put in, things don't seem to go in our favor. To top it off, we get wrongly accused, people judge us, blame us & then try to make us out to be something or someone we're not. This can be so hurtful & frustrating, but what do we do? Is God really in control in the midst of all the chaos? Of course he is. In fact, God sent Paul & Silas to a place where he knew that they would be mistreated & imprisoned. We know Paul wasn't happy about this treatment, he was a Roman citizen after all. At the very least it was frustrating & irritating & unarguably a little scary. All of which are feelings, instead of acting mad, sad or scared, they chose to sing praises to the most high God. They sang until the earth shook & the chains fell off! They made their feelings & thoughts obey God & they created a place for God to dwell because God inhabits our praise, Psalm 22:3. What would have happened if they fought, argued & cried out in fear? The other prisoners were listening to them just like others are watching you & how you act when times get hard. Do you think the jailer & his entire family would have given their lives to Christ? Putting on our breastplate of righteousness is not just for the obvious sins like greed, lust, lying etc; in order to secure our breastplate firmly in place, we must make every feeling & thought obey God, lining our actions up with God's word regardless of how we feel or the circumstances. When we start taking every feeling & thought captive, making them obey God, the earth moves, chains are broken & people start believing & accepting Jesus & that's what it's all about!

WEAPONS ASSIGNMENT

2 CORINTHIANS 10:4-5 The weapons we fight with are not the weapons of the world. On the contrary, they have divine power to demolish strongholds. We demolish arguments & every pretension that sets itself up against the knowledge of God, & we take captive every thought to make it obedient to Christ.

PHASE 6: BREASTPLATE OF RIGHTEOUSNESS
I CAN MAKE MY FEELINGS & THOUGHTS OBEY GOD

COMBAT TRAINING

TELL THE STORY OF PAUL & SILAS IN ACTS 16

When Paul & Silas went to prison, they must have been scared & probably angry since they didn't deserve it because they didn't do anything wrong. Sometimes people mistreat us or call us names & we don't deserve those things at all. We know those unkind things that people say about us aren't true because God made us & only God can say who we are, but mean words & actions can still hurt our feelings & even make us angry & make us think about saying unkind things back. Paul & Silas had those same types of thoughts & feelings, but they chose to make their feelings & thoughts obey God. They praised God. We need to praise God not only when times are good but also when times are hard. They praised God so much that the earth shook & their chains fell off! Obeying God & praising him is how we break free in difficult situations. We can make all our feelings & thoughts obey God by doing the right thing even if it isn't what we are feeling. Do you think the jailer would have given his life to Jesus if Paul & Silas just fought & complained the entire time? When you make your thoughts & feelings obey God, others will notice how you respond & it will help others come to know Jesus.

RECONNAISSANCE

- God knew Paul & Silas would go to prison, but he sent them to the town anyways. Why do you think God would send them there if he knew they would be arrested?

- Paul & Silas were attacked & beaten with rods, but they still praised God. When they were put in prison, they were covered in bruises & cuts from being beaten, but they still praised God. Do you think it might have been hard for them to praise God instead of being angry after this happened?

- It wasn't just one person that was mistreating Paul & Silas but there was an entire crowd of people who wanted them dead & gone. How do you think this made them feel?

- Because they kept praising God & singing God's praises, the earth shook & their chains were broken, but they didn't run away, they stayed & because of their faith & the way they acted, the Jailer accepted Jesus & so did his family. Do you think the Jailer & his family would have accepted Jesus if Paul & Silas acted mad & angry about what was happening to them?

PHASE 6: BREASTPLATE OF RIGHTEOUSNESS
I CAN MAKE MY FEELINGS & THOUGHTS OBEY GOD

THE OBJECTIVE

YOU WILL NEED A box of cake mix, a large mixing bowl & mixing spoon along with random ingredients that you would never mix into a cake such as mustard, tuna, beans & rocks. You will also need a couple of ingredients that the cake recipe calls for such as eggs & water. Bake or buy enough good cupcakes for everyone & have those hidden.

Let everyone know you're going to make them a cake. Pour the cake mix into the bowl & toss the box aside. Why does cake even come with directions? It's so much more fun when you can do whatever you want! Start mixing in the random ingredients one at a time. Engage your audience & ask them what they think of directions & rules. Isn't this so much better? Mix in the eggs & water & let them know that the directions require those ingredients. After all, you want to follow some of the instructions to make sure it tastes good.

WHAT'S THE POINT? Cakes have instructions so they will taste their very best. If we follow only a few parts of the recipe while ignoring the rest & adding in things that don't belong, our cake isn't going to taste very good. The creator of the recipe wants you to enjoy the cake so they made sure to include the perfect instructions for you to follow. God is our creator & he gave us a perfect set of instructions in the Bible because he wants us to enjoy life. God didn't create rules to keep us from having fun. He wants to protect us & keep us from harm. He gave us his word so we could live our best life. God wants us to have fun & enjoy life to the fullest! This is why it is so important that we make every single thought & feeling obey God. If we only obey some of God's ways & ignore others & then start adding things to our lives that don't belong, then our lives won't be so enjoyable anymore & they won't turn out so well in the end. Only when we follow God's recipe for life step by step & obey the Bible word for word will we enjoy our best life.

PHASE 6: BREASTPLATE OF RIGHTEOUSNESS
I CAN MAKE MY FEELINGS & THOUGHTS OBEY GOD

WEAPONS INSPECTION

2 CORINTHIANS 10:4-5 The weapons we fight with are not the weapons of the world. On the contrary, they have divine power to demolish strongholds. We demolish arguments & every pretension that sets itself up against the knowledge of God, & we take captive every thought to make it obedient to Christ.

BREASTPLATE OF RIGHTEOUSNESS: As you probably already know, the Roman soldier's breastplate was worn over his chest & torso area to protect his vital organs such as his heart & lungs, but his breastplate also covered his back & his sides. With the breastplate securely attached to his belt, he was protected from all sides & the enemy would be hard pressed to deliver a fatal blow. When we line our feelings & thoughts up with God's word then we are protected from any attack the enemy throws our way. Sometimes, we feel like giving up because we think we can't do something, but God's word tells us we can do all things through Christ, Philippians 4:13. Sometimes we feel like lashing out in anger because of the unfair treatment we are receiving, but God's word tells us in James 1:19-20 that this behavior is not the righteousness of God. We often feel & think things that are ungodly, this is what temptation is, that's why we must immediately take every thought captive & make it obey God. This is how we put on our breastplate of righteousness. When we have our breastplate of righteousness secured tight to our belt of truth then nothing can touch us, God has us covered from the front, the back & all sides including our future & our past!

PHASE 6: BREASTPLATE OF RIGHTEOUSNESS
I CAN MAKE MY FEELINGS & THOUGHTS OBEY GOD

THE MISSION

TO COMPLETE YOUR MISSION YOU WILL NEED THE FOLLOWING WEAPON FROM THE BIBLE: 2 CORINTHIANS 10:4-5 The weapons we fight with are not the weapons of the world. On the contrary, they have divine power to demolish strongholds. We demolish arguments & every pretension that sets itself up against the knowledge of God, & we take captive every thought to make it obedient to Christ.

YOUR MISSION: PUT ON YOUR BREASTPLATE OF RIGHTEOUSNESS! To do this you must make every feeling & thought obey God. Remember that God gave you a perfect set of instructions in his word, the Bible.

WATCH FOR TRAPS: You can't control everything that happens in life, but you can control how you choose to respond. Sometimes people will be unkind & unfair things will happen in life. This can leave you feeling sad or mad. Feeling sad or mad isn't wrong but we should never choose how we act or what we say based on how we feel. We can always respond in a way that is obedient & pleasing to God.

DEFEAT THE ENEMY: When someone or something makes you sad or mad, instead of reacting, pray about your thoughts & feelings. Ask God to help you act in a way that pleases him. Remember, your feelings & thoughts don't control you. You control your feelings & thoughts. Take every thought & feeling that you have & make it obey God by acting & speaking in a way that is pleasing to him. You are stronger than any thought or feeling you have & God is with you every step of the way!

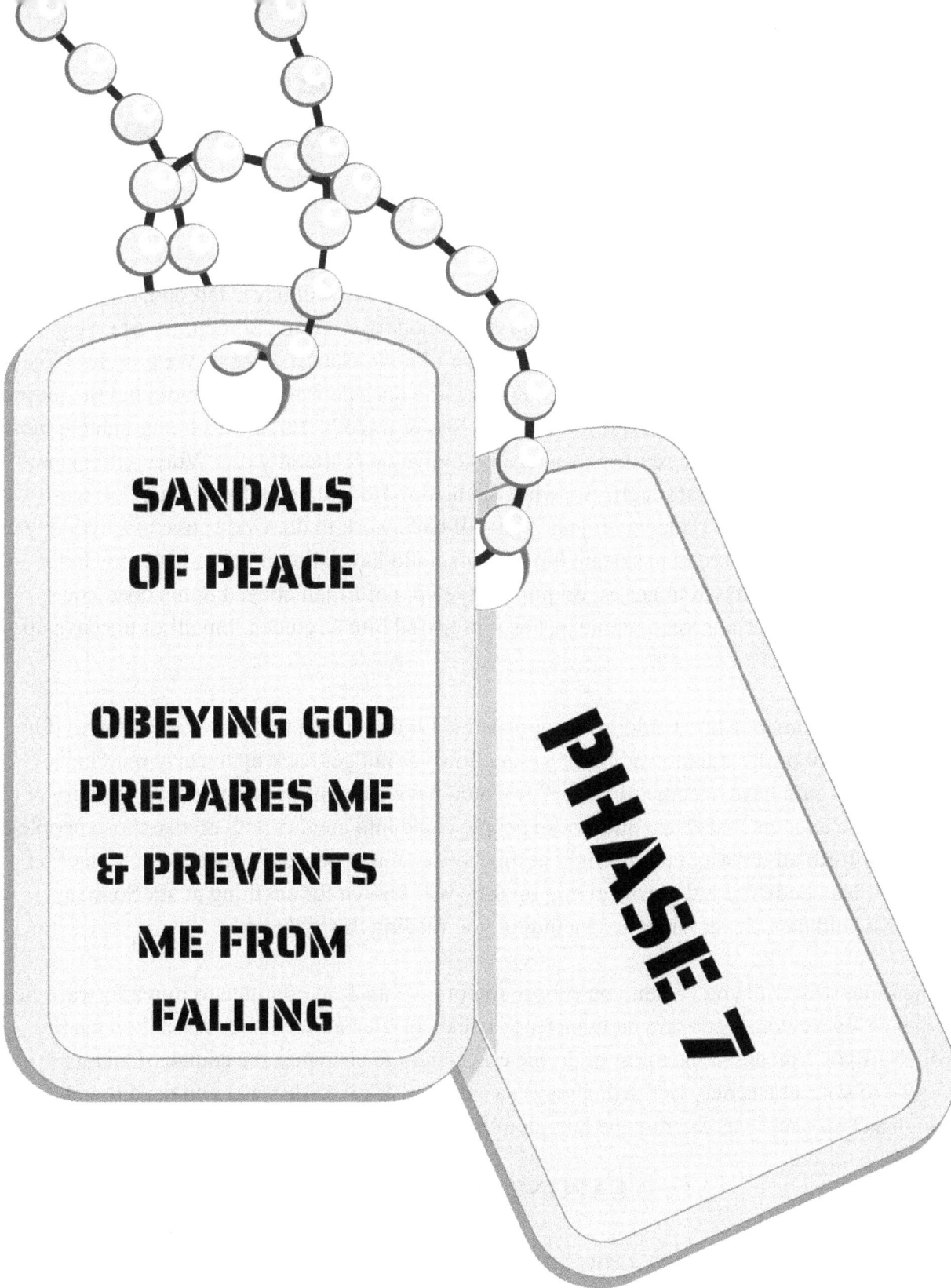

SANDALS OF PEACE

OBEYING GOD PREPARES ME & PREVENTS ME FROM FALLING

PHASE 7

PHASE 7: SANDALS OF PEACE
OBEYING GOD PREPARES ME & PREVENTS ME FROM FALLING

BATTLE PREP

READ 1 KINGS 19

Okay, real talk, just because we're Christians doesn't mean we will never fall on hard times or get tired or simply feel like we've had enough & can no longer go on. Sometimes life overwhelms us & there are times where we just don't know what to do next. We pray for God to open the doors he wants us to walk through & close the ones he wants us to avoid but the journey can get tough. Some of us have experienced great loss & tragedy. Elijah was being hunted, most of his friends had been murdered & he was ready to give up & literally die. Who could blame him after what he had been through? So, what did he do? He laid down to die, but God wasn't done with him & God isn't done with you. You still have work to do. God spoke to Elijah & gave him the sustenance he needed to sustain him. Elijah could have chosen not to listen to God's word; he could have chosen to not eat & quit & give up, but Elijah obeyed & his obedience prepared him for what was yet to come just as it prepared him & guided him all of his days up until that point.

Imagine for a moment what would have happened if Elijah refused to follow God's word, if he took himself out of the equation & chose to stay down & not get back up to carry out God's work. What would have become of Elisha? It would have had a profound impact on history & all the people he encountered & the ones those people came into contact with & also those people & so on & so forth all the way up until right at this very moment because he would no longer be known for his obedience but for his giving up if he was known for anything at all. So many miracles would have never happened including you reading this right now.

It's the same way with you. When you choose to not give up & to continue to move forward in obedience, every young person you minister to is like an Elisha hearing God's call on his life through Elijah. You are in the midst of divine encounters & changing the course of history. Because of your obedience, God will always sustain you & give you what you need to get through as you alter lives & grow the Kingdom.

WEAPONS ASSIGNMENT

PSALMS 119:105 Your word is a lamp to my feet, a light on my path.

PHASE 7: SANDALS OF PEACE
OBEYING GOD PREPARES ME & PREVENTS ME FROM FALLING

COMBAT TRAINING

TELL THE STORY OF ELIJAH BY THE BROOK WITH THE RAVENS & THE WIDOW & HER OIL & FLOUR IN 1 KINGS 17:1-16

Elijah listened to the word of God & always obeyed what God told him to do & because of this he was always prepared for anything that happened. When so many other people in the land were starving & dying of thirst, Elijah had food to eat & water to drink. Elijah did what God told him & went where God told him & when God sent him to the widow & her son, she could have refused to listen to the man of God, but she chose to obey & obeying God's word saved her & her son. God's word doesn't always make sense to people in the world who are chasing after worldly things, but the only true way to be prepared for everything & anything is by knowing & obeying God's word because only God truly knows the future & what is yet to come.

RECONNAISSANCE

- Elijah lived a very long time ago but much like today, he lived in a time where others were disobedient to God, however, Elijah obeyed God & because he obeyed God, he was prepared for the drought & the famine & was able to eat & drink while others starved. What do you think would have happened to Elijah if he didn't obey God?

- When the brook dried up & God told Elijah to move on, he probably wasn't thrilled about the long journey to another town, but he obeyed God. Sometimes, we have work to do that we don't want to do & things change when we don't want them to. We know what would have happened to Elijah if he didn't move on because there wasn't any water left, but what about the people he was sent to help. What would have happened to the widow & her son if Elijah disobeyed God?

- It may have seemed ridiculous for Elijah to ask the widow for her very last bite of food, but if she denied Elijah, it probably would have been her last bite. However, because she obeyed the word of God & put God first, she had everything she needed.

- If Elijah didn't spend time with God by praying & learning God's word, Elijah would have never heard God's voice or knew what God wanted him to do next & that wouldn't have only been bad for Elijah but also the people God sent Elijah to help. When you take the time & do the work to learn God's word & choose to obey it, this not only prepares you for anything but it will also have a great impact on other people because you will be able to speak God's word to them & tell them about Jesus so they may be saved.

PHASE 7: SANDALS OF PEACE
OBEYING GOD PREPARES ME & PREVENTS ME FROM FALLING

THE OBJECTIVE

YOU WILL NEED A newspaper.

Let the kids know you're going on a trip & a lot of roads had to be closed because they became too dangerous to drive on & some of them are so dangerous that you could drive right off a cliff, but the newspaper has a list of all the roads you need to avoid. Also, there is a huge dangerous storm that will be swooping in & the newspaper is your only source to find out what direction you need to go to avoid the storm. Also, because of the storm, a lot of the & grocery stores will be closed & if you don't look at the newspaper, you will get stuck on the road in the path of the storm without any gas or food or water. Fumble through the newspaper & then toss it in the trash. Reading the newspaper takes up too much time! I will just go on my trip & guess which way to go.

Ask everyone if they think you should read the newspaper to prepare for your trip. Ask them why. Tell them you will have other people in the car with you too. Ask them if they think you should do what the newspaper says since it is the only real source of information to keep you safe & prepare you on your journey.

WHAT'S THE POINT? This is how it is on our journey through life. We have God's word to prepare us & keep us safe, but what if we don't read it? What if we don't take the time to learn God's word. What if we refuse to obey it? Remember, God has work for us to do & people who need to be rescued by hearing the word of God. We don't have to be afraid of anything that may happen in this life when we have Jesus guiding us, we will always have peace & be unafraid because knowing & obeying God's word prepares us for anything & prevents us from falling into temptation & going the wrong way.

WEAPONS INSPECTION

PSALMS 119:105 Your word is a lamp to my feet, a light on my path.

SANDALS OF PEACE: God's word tells us to shod our feet with the preparation of the gospel of peace. To shod means to fit perfectly so it doesn't slip or come off. The Roman soldiers tied their sandals to their feet just like we bind ourselves to God's word by obeying it. The Roman soldiers' sandals had sharp spikes on the bottom of them to help them stand firm & not slip but those spikes also helped them to defend against the enemy just like knowing & obeying God's word defends & protects us. By knowing & obeying God's word, we are prepared & we won't fall into temptation because we are tied to the perfect will of God. When we take the time to learn God's word then follow it in obedience, God guides us & lights the way.

PHASE 7: SANDALS OF PEACE
OBEYING GOD PREPARES ME & PREVENTS ME FROM FALLING

THE MISSION

TO COMPLETE YOUR MISSION YOU WILL NEED THE FOLLOWING WEAPON FROM THE BIBLE:PSALMS 119:105 Your word is a lamp to my feet, a light on my path.

YOUR MISSION: PUT ON THE SANDALS OF PEACE! Prepare yourself by learning your Bible verses & always obeying God's word.

WATCH FOR TRAPS: When you're faced with a problem or a situation that is unpleasant to you, make sure you respond in a way that is pleasing to God. Don't fear or get discouraged. Allow God to guide you through every hard situation by obeying his word.

DEFEAT THE ENEMY: Keep learning & obeying God's word. Don't forget to pray & read your Bible verse every day. You can also choose to read a little more each day & talk to God more often. God loves you & wants to hear from you! Knowing & obeying God's word will prepare you for anything. Nothing can stop you now!

SHIELD OF
FAITH

I KNOW
GOD WILL
ALWAYS KEEP
HIS WORD

PHASE 8

PHASE 8: SHIELD OF FAITH
I KNOW GOD WILL ALWAYS KEEP HIS WORD

BATTLE PREP

READ HEBREWS 11

Wow! There's no wonder why Hebrews 11 is known as the faith chapter. God did all of that & so much more! There is no way to list or put into words all the wonderful, marvelous, miraculous things that God has done. From the foundations of the universe, all the miracles in the Bible, everything Jesus did, the work of the disciples, all of the healing, personal testimonies & every answered prayer, right up to you reading this right now because this is one of my answered prayers. I know that you already know how incredible God is & that he is fully capable of absolutely anything. I know you believe God did it & he can do it, but do you believe that he will do it for you? After everything that we know about God, after all the miracles we've read about, have seen & even experienced, sometimes we can still struggle with knowing that he will do it & that he will do it again & again because he is unchanging & never failing & his love for us doesn't run out & he has no limits. We can never deplete his wonder working power!

Peter walked with Jesus & saw the incredible power of God & he didn't hesitate to step out of the boat onto the waves of the raging sea & walk on water to Jesus. Peter believed Jesus was fully capable but when he took his eyes off of Jesus & started looking at the storm, he began to sink & he didn't know if God would give him that same power to walk on the water. You believe God is fully capable of doing anything you ask in Jesus name, but do you know without doubting that God will for you? When we keep our eyes on Jesus, there is no room for doubt but when we start to look at the storm, all the things that tell us it is impossible, that's when we start to sink. When we use our shield of faith, we can extinguish every lie the enemy throws our way to make us doubt God's faithfulness: ~~God can for others but he won't for me, I don't deserve it, I'm not good enough, I've tried & failed too many times, I'm not as good as them, I'm not chosen, I know what I did in my past, I'll look foolish for believing that~~. Keep your eyes on Jesus & don't believe the storm of lies! God can & God will for you! God always keeps his word.

WEAPONS ASSIGNMENT

HEBREWS 11:1 Now faith is confidence in what we hope for & assurance about what we do not see.

PHASE 8: SHIELD OF FAITH
I KNOW GOD WILL ALWAYS KEEP HIS WORD

COMBAT TRAINING

TELL THE STORY OF JESUS & PETER WALKING ON THE WATER IN MATTHEW 14

Imagine it, you're on a boat in the middle of a raging sea, your boat is taking on water, you're already scared & thinking you're going to die & then you see someone walking on the water! It's a ghost! That's exactly what the disciples thought & they were so terrified that they started screaming. The same men who have been with Jesus day & night & have performed miracles & cast out demons were now terrified of a storm & what they thought to be a ghost. It wasn't a spirit, it was Jesus & he told them to cheer up & stop being afraid. Peter was the only one who stepped out in faith, but not before he asked & Jesus told him to, which is a good thing because we always have to make sure our actions line up with God's word. Stepping out on to the crashing waves, Peter looked at Jesus & got closer to him with each step but then Peter started to look at the waves crashing around him & he felt the wind gusting & he must have had a million thoughts running through his mind telling him this was crazy & he was about to drown or die or both. Peter began to sink. Once Peter took his eyes off of Jesus & started looking at the storm instead of Jesus, he started believing every doubtful & fearful thought until he almost drowned. Peter cried out for Jesus to save him & of course Jesus did. Jesus reached down & rescued him while telling Peter that he didn't have enough faith & he had too much doubt. Peter learned a valuable lesson & taught us one too. We have to keep our eyes on Jesus without doubting or being fearful, always trusting in God's promises. We can't let negative thoughts creep in telling us that we can't. We know God can & we have to keep believing that God will do for us what he said he would. Faith isn't believing God can; faith is knowing God will. God will always keep his word.

PHASE 8: SHIELD OF FAITH
I KNOW GOD WILL ALWAYS KEEP HIS WORD

RECONNAISSANCE

- The disciples already knew Jesus & had seen him perform all sorts of healings & miracles. After all of this, they were still afraid in the storm when they could no longer see Jesus. We can't see Jesus, but he is always with us. What are some things that we can do each day to keep ourselves connected with God so we don't forget he is with us?

- What was the first thing Jesus commanded the disciples to do when he saw them afraid in the boat? Cheer up! The second thing? Don't be afraid! To the world, it seems ridiculous to be of good cheer when problems arise, but we know fear comes from doubt & unbelief. When you have faith in God, you can rejoice because you know God is with you, protecting you & working on your behalf. You can get through the storm with good cheer knowing God is taking care of every problem & working it all out for your good. We don't ever need to be afraid.

- What did Peter do before he stepped out of the boat? He asked Jesus & didn't step out until Jesus told him to. It's important for us to pray & ask Jesus what he wants us to do. God gives us his word, the Bible, to help us do exactly what he wants us to do. If something does not line up with God's word completely then we don't do it. By praying & reading God's word, we can increase our faith in God & learn to hear God's voice in every storm & recognize it from all others.

- Why did Peter start to sink? He took his eyes off Jesus. He looked at the storm & this made him afraid. He heard every thought in his mind telling him how impossible this was & he became afraid. What are some thoughts & feelings you have that make you feel afraid? How can we keep our eyes on Jesus? Peter knew Jesus could walk on water. Peter also knew that he could walk on water if God gave him the ability because Peter was already doing it but Peter began to doubt God would continue to do it & he became afraid & started sinking. Faith isn't believing God can; faith is knowing God will for us. God will always keep his word. Do you think Peter failed? Why or why not? He was the only disciple who even tried & he also learned a valuable lesson & taught us one too. Even though Peter struggled with his faith, it took faith to walk on water for even a second. Do you think the experience increased Peter's faith? Do you think Peter should have stayed in the boat? What are some things God wants you to do that you're afraid to try? Fear never comes from God. You never have to be afraid because Jesus is always with you. God's Holy Spirit lives inside of you. When you trust in God & keep your eyes on Jesus, there isn't anything that you cannot do.

PHASE 8: SHIELD OF FAITH
I KNOW GOD WILL ALWAYS KEEP HIS WORD

THE OBJECTIVE

YOU WILL NEED A lamp with a light bulb.

Leave the bulb unscrewed just enough to not turn on when you plug in the lamp. Have the lamp visibly unplugged & try to turn it on. Why isn't it working? It isn't going to work if it isn't connected to the power source. It should work once it's plugged in. What? It's still not working. What could be the issue? The light bulb isn't fully connected. Once it is plugged in with the bulb securely in place then all we need to do is flip the switch & turn it on without even thinking about it. It works every time!

WHAT'S THE POINT? When we flip a switch to turn on the lights, we believe that the light is going to come on. If we didn't believe it, we wouldn't flip the switch. However, there are certain things that need to be properly in place before the light will work. The light must be connected to a power source & the bulb must be fully connected or it won't work. This is how it is with our faith. God is the power source that we need to plug in to. We do this by reading our Bible, obeying God's word & connecting with God through prayer. We believe what God tells us & we obey it. When we have faith in God, we can ask him for anything according to his will, & if it lines up with his word, then God will do it for us as long as we believe.

WEAPONS INSPECTION

HEBREWS 11:1 Now faith is confidence in what we hope for & assurance about what we do not see.

SHIELD OF FAITH: God tells us to carry our shield of faith with us everywhere. Faith is believing everything that God tells us in his word & knowing that God will always do what he says he will do. The Roman soldiers had a shield that protected them against the attacks of their enemies. It was as big as a small door that curved around them & protected them. It also had a big piece of metal on the front that would protect their hand & kept them from dropping it if an enemy struck. That same piece of metal could also be used to knock out the enemy. The shield was made from pieces of wood layered together & covered in leather. Before battle, the soldiers would soak their shields in water. They did this because the enemy often attacked with arrows that were on fire, but their shields would put out all the flames. When the enemy attacks us lies & tries to tell us we aren't good enough, smart enough, strong enough or can't do something that God tells us that we can do, we have our shield of faith in God & we trust in what God says about us & we put out all those fiery darts telling us lies about ourselves. We take our shield of faith with us everywhere we go & we don't just believe that God can do something for us, we know he will do everything he has said he will do. God will always keep his word.

PHASE 8: SHIELD OF FAITH
I KNOW GOD WILL ALWAYS KEEP HIS WORD

THE MISSION

TO COMPLETE YOUR MISSION YOU WILL NEED THE FOLLOWING WEAPON FROM THE BIBLE: HEBREWS 11:1 Now faith is confidence in what we hope for & assurance about what we do not see.

YOUR MISSION: CARRY YOUR SHIELD OF FAITH WITH YOU EVERYWHERE! Never doubt that God will always keep his word & that you can do everything that God has called you to do.

WATCH FOR TRAPS: Anything that makes you doubt God is a trap. God's word is always true. God will always do what he said he will do. He is always with you & working things out for your good. Don't believe anyone or any thought that makes you doubt God's love & faithfulness.

DEFEAT THE ENEMY: Obey God, keep your eyes on Jesus & keep walking towards him & nothing will sink you! Learn your Bible verse, pray & read your Bible. Reading your Bible will strengthen your faith & help you get closer to God & know him in a special, personal way. Know that God will do everything he said he would do for you. Yes, you! God loves you & cares about you so very much. Even if things don't seem like they are working out, God is working things out for your good. Jesus is there with you when things get hard. Don't look at all the obstacles, problems & troubles telling you it's impossible. Keep your eyes on Jesus without doubting & let God guide you every step of the way. Your faith in God is amazing! Nothing can stop you from doing what God wants you to do!

HELMET OF
SALVATION

FILLING MY MIND
WITH GOD'S
WORD RENEWS
& PROTECTS
MY MIND

PHASE 9

PHASE 9: HELMET OF SALVATION
FILLING MY MIND WITH GOD'S WORD RENEWS & PROTECTS MY MIND

BATTLE PREP

READ LUKE 4

We know God will never tempt us (James 1:13-16); however, God will allow us to be tempted, Remember Job? That ugly ol' satan was just wandering about & God was like, hey satan, look at Job (Job 1:7-8), check out Job! Why in the world? For God's glory & for our good. Every time we overcome temptation, we become stronger & more empowered. Our desires become more aligned with God. Resisting temptation makes satan run (James 4:7)! God led Jesus into the wilderness & it was there that Jesus was tempted. He was hungry, his mind & body were weakened & fatigued. He was battling thoughts within his mind. He was tempted physically with bread. He was tempted emotionally, satan wanted him to question God's love for him & make Jesus doubt who he was. He was tempted with control, greed & pride. Jesus could have it all if he would just bow down to satan. His father already owned it all & it was already his! Every single time Jesus was tempted, he spoke God's word. Why? Was it to remind satan what God's word said? No. Dirty boy satan already knew God's word. Jesus was renewing his own mind by meditating on God's word, speaking God's word, praying God's word, reminding himself of God's word & fixing his focus on God. After all, when we are tempted, it all starts in the mind. The battle takes place in the mind & that's where we must overcome it & immediately eradicate it with God's word so it doesn't give birth to sin. When we are tempted, we can rejoice because the trying of our faith works patience which increases our endurance which strengthens our faith & renews our mind (James 1:2-3).

WEAPONS ASSIGNMENT

ROMANS 12:2 Do not conform to the pattern of this world, but be transformed by the renewing of your mind. Then you will be able to test & approve what God's will is - his good, pleasing & perfect will.

COMBAT TRAINING

TELL THE STORY OF THE TEMPTATION OF JESUS IN LUKE 4

When satan showed up, Jesus hadn't eaten so his body was becoming weak & tired, but Jesus kept his mind renewed & strong by praying to God & thinking about God's word. Ever since Jesus was a young boy, he spent a lot of time learning & memorizing God's word. Since Jesus knew God's word, he knew the exact scriptures to pray & to speak to fight off every temptation. It's not a sin to be tempted. You're tempted when you have a thought that is against God's word. It's only a sin if you act on the thought. A simple example would be stealing. Let's say you see something you want & you think for a brief second that nobody is looking & you can take it & nobody would know. That is temptation. You know stealing is wrong because the Bible tells us not to steal, so you choose to do the right thing & not sin. It wasn't a sin to be tempted. It would only be a sin if you took it. That's simple enough. However, sometimes we can have thoughts that make us feel bad about ourselves or doubt God's love for us. We might have a thought that tells us nobody loves us & we are all alone, but we can fight off the temptation to believe those lies with God's word because the Bible tells us that God loves us & he is always with us & he will never leave us or forsake us. What if we feel like we're ugly & we don't have a purpose in life? If we know our Bible, then we know that's a lie from the devil because the Bible tells us that we are God's beautiful masterpiece & God has prepared good works for us to do & he has a purpose & plan for our lives. Instead of listening to the lies of satan, we can pray & thank God that he created us in Christ Jesus & tell God that we know he has a purpose & plan for our life & ask him to reveal it to us. When we learn God's word & know our Bible verses, this keeps our mind strong & renewed so when the devil tries to tempt us or make us believe things that are against God's word, we will know God's word & know what's right according to God. We can pray God's word & speak God's word & pray to God about his promises & ask him to show us things about ourselves & his word. When we are doing this, it leaves no room for the devil to trick us into believing things about ourselves that aren't true. We are too busy believing in God & renewing our minds so stan has no choice but to leave us alone & run away like a little coward.

WEAPONS ASSIGNMENT

ROMANS 12:2 Do not conform to the pattern of this world, but be transformed by the renewing of your mind. Then you will be able to test & approve what God's will is - his good, pleasing & perfect will.

PHASE 9: HELMET OF SALVATION
FILLING MY MIND WITH GOD'S WORD RENEWS & PROTECTS MY MIND

RECONNAISSANCE

- God knew Jesus would be tempted by satan when he was led into the wilderness. Why do you think God allows us to be tempted? Every time we overcome a temptation, it makes us stronger.

- Jesus was tempted in three ways: physically with food, emotionally by satan trying to make him doubt himself & doubt God's love for him & with control by trying to convince Jesus he could have the entire world if he bowed down. Jesus never sinned & was able to overcome every temptation with the word of God that he had been learning & studying since he was a boy. What do you think would have happened if Jesus never learned his Bible verses?

- When Jesus spoke God's word back to satan, it wasn't to convince satan of God's word because satan already knew the Bible. That's right, satan knows the Bible inside & out but he doesn't obey it. So, if satan already knew God's word, then who benefited from Jesus speaking God's word? Do you think it helped Jesus to pray & to hear God's word?

- Do you think you know enough Bible verses to fight off every temptation or do you think you should keep renewing your mind while learning as many Bible verses as you can?

PHASE 9: HELMET OF SALVATION
FILLING MY MIND WITH GOD'S WORD RENEWS & PROTECTS MY MIND

THE OBJECTIVE

YOU WILL NEED fresh fruits & vegetables of different colors & a glass of water.

We know drinking water & eating fruits & vegetables helps us stay healthy. Take a small bite of one of the vegetables & a small sip of water & say you never have to take another sip of water or eat another bite of fruits & vegetables ever again. Ask everyone if they agree it works like this.

WHAT'S THE POINT? We have to drink plenty of water & eat fruits & vegetables each day to stay healthy, grow strong & build our immune system so our body can protect us from sicknesses. Different fruits & vegetables have different types of benefits to nourish & protect different parts of our body. Eating one bite or taking one sip isn't going to be enough to stay healthy for life. We need water every day to live, Without water we die. Without Jesus we die & sure, we may be able to get into Heaven without knowing many Bible verses just like you may be able to survive without eating many fruits & vegetables, but you will never be as strong. There are Bible verses for every problem & situation in life. The more Bible verses we fill our mind with & let it get down into our hearts by obeying each one, the more our mind becomes renewed & protected. We will know how to respond in every situation because we know what God's word says about it. Just as we need healthy food & water every single day, we need God's word every single day & the more of it we get, the stronger & more protected our mind becomes.

WEAPONS INSPECTION

ROMANS 12:2 Do not conform to the pattern of this world, but be transformed by the renewing of your mind. Then you will be able to test & approve what God's will is - his good, pleasing & perfect will.

HELMET OF SALVATION: The Roman helmet was originally made of leather & as you can imagine, leather didn't work too well, so they switched to various metals that protected their head much better. If they continued to do things in the same way or if they did what the other armies were doing, they would have been quickly defeated. Making the most of their helmets, Roman soldiers would polish them until they shined & then march directly into the sun. As the enemy advanced towards them, all they could see was helmets like mirrors reflecting the sun back to them, blinding them & rendering them powerless. Unable to see, the enemy would often turn & run. When we know & pray God's word, our minds are protected from every lie & temptation. When we polish up on God's word by learning, praying & speaking it, our minds become renewed & we can put on our helmets of salvation, march boldly towards the Son of God, blinding the enemy & making him turn & run because as he comes towards us, all he will see is Jesus shining back at him!

PHASE 9: HELMET OF SALVATION
FILLING MY MIND WITH GOD'S WORD RENEWS & PROTECTS MY MIND

THE MISSION

TO COMPLETE YOUR MISSION YOU WILL NEED THE FOLLOWING WEAPON FROM THE BIBLE: ROMANS 12:2 Do not conform to the pattern of this world, but be transformed by the renewing of your mind. Then you will be able to test & approve what God's will is - his good, pleasing & perfect will.

YOUR MISSION: POLISH YOUR HELMET OF SALVATION UNTIL IT SHINES! Learn your Bible verses, think about them, pray about them & speak God's word out loud. Declare that you will never conform to this world. Instead, you will always obey God's word.

WATCH FOR TRAPS: Sometimes you'll have feelings that might make you doubt God's word or make you feel silly for speaking it. Crush those thoughts as soon as they enter your mind & don't believe the lies of the enemy. It's not silly to speak God's word, it renews & protects your mind & makes you strong.

DEFEAT THE ENEMY: Blind the enemy with your bright, shiny helmet of salvation! As you continue to fill your mind up with God's word, your mind will become renewed & protected from every lie & temptation. You'll know what is pleasing to God & you will choose to obey God's word. As you respond to every situation in a godly manner, this will make you shine with the light of Jesus, blinding your enemy & making him run. You are a strong & mighty warrior for Jesus!

SWORD OF
THE SPIRIT

SPEAKING
GOD'S WORD
MAKES GREAT
THINGS HAPPEN

PHASE 10

PHASE 10: SWORD OF THE SPIRIT
SPEAKING GOD'S WORD MAKES GREAT THINGS HAPPEN

BATTLE PREP

READ MARK 11

God created the entire universe with only his word. God's word is quick & powerful & sharper than any two-edged sword, Hebrews 4:12. When we speak God's word in faith, we can make great things happen. God made us in his image & gave us dominion over the Earth. For us to shape our world & make great things happen, we have to speak God's word out loud, sending it out & commanding it what to do. Jesus said, "…I say unto you, that whosoever *say* unto this mountain, be thou removed, be thou cast into the sea; & shall not doubt in his heart, but shall believe that those things which he *saith* shall come to pass; he shall have whatever he *saith*.", Mark 11:23. Jesus didn't tell us to just silently pray but to speak our prayer in faith without doubt. Faith cometh by hearing & hearing by the word of God, Romans 10:17. Since faith comes by hearing then we must speak God's word out loud so it can accomplish what we want it to do. Does this mean we can have anything we want if we only speak & believe it while we pray in faith? When it lines up with the perfect, infallible word of God, then yes. When we speak God's word, we are exercising the authority given to us by God & occupying territory that has already been won. In verse 24 Jesus tells us, what things soever ye desire, when ye pray, believe that ye receive them, & ye shall have them. However, in verse 25, Jesus goes on to tell us to make sure we forgive anyone that we have not yet forgiven so our Father in Heaven can forgive us. Forgiving others is so important because we must do it in order to be forgiven, & our salvation & freedom comes through receiving forgiveness. Jame 5:16 tells us that a prayer of a righteous person is effective, so for our prayer to be effective we must forgive & be forgiven. When we are righteous by God's standards & line up our wants & desires with God's word & perfect will, we can wield God's word & make great things happen.

WEAPONS ASSIGNMENT

JAMES 3:10-12 Out of the same mouth come praise & cursing. My brothers & sisters, this should not be. Can both fresh water & salt water flow from the same spring? My brothers & sisters, can a fig tree bear olives, or a grapevine bear figs? Neither can a salt spring produce fresh water.

PHASE 10: SWORD OF THE SPIRIT
SPEAKING GOD'S WORD MAKES GREAT THINGS HAPPEN

COMBAT TRAINING

TELL THE STORY OF JESUS CURSING THE FIG TREE IN MARK 11
Why would Jesus curse a tree when the Bible tells us that it wasn't the season for figs to be growing. Think about it. Jesus killed that tree with his words. Why? Do you think he was just hungry & angry? Hangry? No, Jesus did this so he could teach us a valuable lesson. Our words are powerful. What we choose to speak matters & makes a difference. Jesus wanted us to know how powerful our words really are. God's word is perfect & full of promises & when we speak God's word, it accomplishes great things. God's word heals, protects, provides, brings joy & peace & so much more. However, when we pray for something & speak God's word then grumble & complain about the thing we are praying for or praying to change, then that cancels out what we asked for in prayer. If someone is praying for their fiances to change but going around constantly saying how poor they are then they are speaking a curse on themselves just like Jesus did on the fig tree. If Jesus was just hangry then he could have easily commanded the fig tree to produce big, juicy figs. The disciples already knew Jesus could perform miracles. Jesus wanted us to show us that we have to be very careful with our words & how powerful they are. The negative things we say when we complain have an effect, but when we speak God's word, it is a powerful weapon against the enemy. Speaking God's word makes great things happen!

RECONNAISSANCE

- Why would Jesus curse a tree instead of just commanding it to make figs? He wanted to show us how powerful our words are, even the negative ones.

- What are some things that you would like to see God change in your life? Do you ever complain about them? From now on, speak only God's word over these things.

- What was the first thing Jesus said to Peter when he noticed the dead tree? Have faith in God! With faith we can move mountains. Literally! Do we really have faith if we are complaining about the situation? We're joyful when we truly believe.

- Jesus tells us to forgive others. This is so important for us so we can heal from hurt & move on & it is also necessary for God to forgive us. Forgiving others is an important factor in having our prayers answered. Is there anyone that you need to forgive? Let's take a moment to pray & ask God to show us if there is any unforgiveness in our hearts & for God to help us forgive & move on. Remember, the other person doesn't need to be sorry for us to forgive them. We can forgive & be obedient to God no matter how the other person feels or chooses to behave.

PHASE 10: SWORD OF THE SPIRIT
SPEAKING GOD'S WORD MAKES GREAT THINGS HAPPEN

THE OBJECTIVE

YOU WILL NEED a jar such as a Mason jar & enough colorful beads (you can also use coins, candy, rocks, etc) to fill it.

Explain that you really want to fill the jar up to the top & would like some help. Give out half of the beads to the children so they can place them in the jar for you. Emphasize that you really want to fill the jar. It's starting to get there. Have more children come up & instruct them to take out a few beads until it is almost empty. Let them know how much you want the jar to become full, & then once again repeat the process of having children place beads in the jar until it's almost full, then have other children come & remove the beads until it's nearly empty. Keep letting them know how much you want the jar to be full. Dump out the rest of the beads while saying you don't believe the jar will ever get full.

WHAT'S THE POINT? We can make great things happen by speaking God's word. God has a word & a promise for every situation in our lives. We can speak healing & peace into our lives. When we speak God's word, we are commanding angels & spiritual forces to go to work for us, but when we complain & speak our negative thoughts out loud that is also sending instructions that counteract the good we have been praying for. Jesus didn't command someone to be healed then say they are so sick, look how sick they are, I don't think they can ever get better. David didn't pray to defeat the giant then complain about how big & scary the giant was. When we speak God's word, we can accomplish great & mighty things, but we have to be careful not to be discouraged & start complaining when our prayers aren't answered quickly enough. We can't send out mixed signals with our words like I did with the beads. I wanted the jar full but I gave two sets of instructions & then when it was almost full I gave up & dumped it out. Some prayers take time & we need to be patient, but if we start complaining & choose to believe our doubts then we may never see our prayers answered. God doesn't move in our timing, we have to be patient & wait for him to work. We have to trust God to know what is best for every person involved because God loves us so very much & he sees things we cannot. God sees every detail & even knows the future. When we speak God's word & his promises, we have to be careful not to let anything that contradicts that come out of our mouth. Speaking God's word makes great things happen!

PHASE 10: SWORD OF THE SPIRIT
SPEAKING GOD'S WORD MAKES GREAT THINGS HAPPEN

WEAPONS INSPECTION

JAMES 3:10-12 Out of the same mouth come praise & cursing. My brothers & sisters, this should not be. Can both fresh water & salt water flow from the same spring? My brothers & sisters, can a fig tree bear olives, or a grapevine bear figs? Neither can a salt spring produce fresh water.

SWORD OF THE SPIRIT: When you think of a sword fit for battle, you might think of something long & heavy & difficult to wield. However, this wasn't true for the most successful sword of its time. The gladius the Roman soldiers carried was fairly short & light. This made it much more efficient in close combat & in long, drawn out battles than a longer, heavier sword. The sword also had a pommel at the end that not only kept the hand from slipping & balanced the sword to make it feel even lighter, but it could also be used to deliver a deadly blow to the enemy with blunt force. The blade was kept razor sharp on both sides & the tip came to a severe point that would instantly pierce through anything it met. God's word isn't heavy or difficult for us to carry. It's the perfect weapon when the enemy gets close. Speaking God's word strengthens our faith & wins every battle. God's word never fails! The pommel of God's word keeps our life in perfect balance & takes the weight off us & gives each battle to the Lord. All we have to do is speak God's word in faith, believe it without doubting & live in obedience to it & God does all the fighting & heavy lifting for us. Through Jesus, the victory is already ours!

PHASE 10: SWORD OF THE SPIRIT
SPEAKING GOD'S WORD MAKES GREAT THINGS HAPPEN

THE MISSION

TO COMPLETE YOUR MISSION YOU WILL NEED THE FOLLOWING WEAPON FROM THE BIBLE: JAMES 3:10-12 Out of the same mouth come praise & cursing. My brothers & sisters, this should not be. Can both fresh water & salt water flow from the same spring? My brothers & sisters, can a fig tree bear olives, or a grapevine bear figs? Neither can a salt spring produce fresh water.

YOUR MISSION: WEILD YOUR SWORD! Only speak God's word over yourself, your life, others & every situation. God's word will slash through every problem & negative thought & win every battle.

WATCH FOR TRAPS: Some things are undeniably bad, but instead of saying how bad it is, pray about it & speak God's word over the situation. Tell God out loud that you trust him & you know he can solve your problem. You won't always understand why something is happening but continue to tell God you trust him & you know he holds your future. Pray for wisdom, pray for strength & pray for your future. Speak good things out loud about yourself, your life & others.

DEFEAT THE ENEMY: Let only good & positive things flow from your mouth. Remember, your words are instructions & they have power. Don't complain. Keep trusting God because he loves you so very much. Keep praying & learning your Bible verses because it's God's word. Speaking God's word makes great things happen!

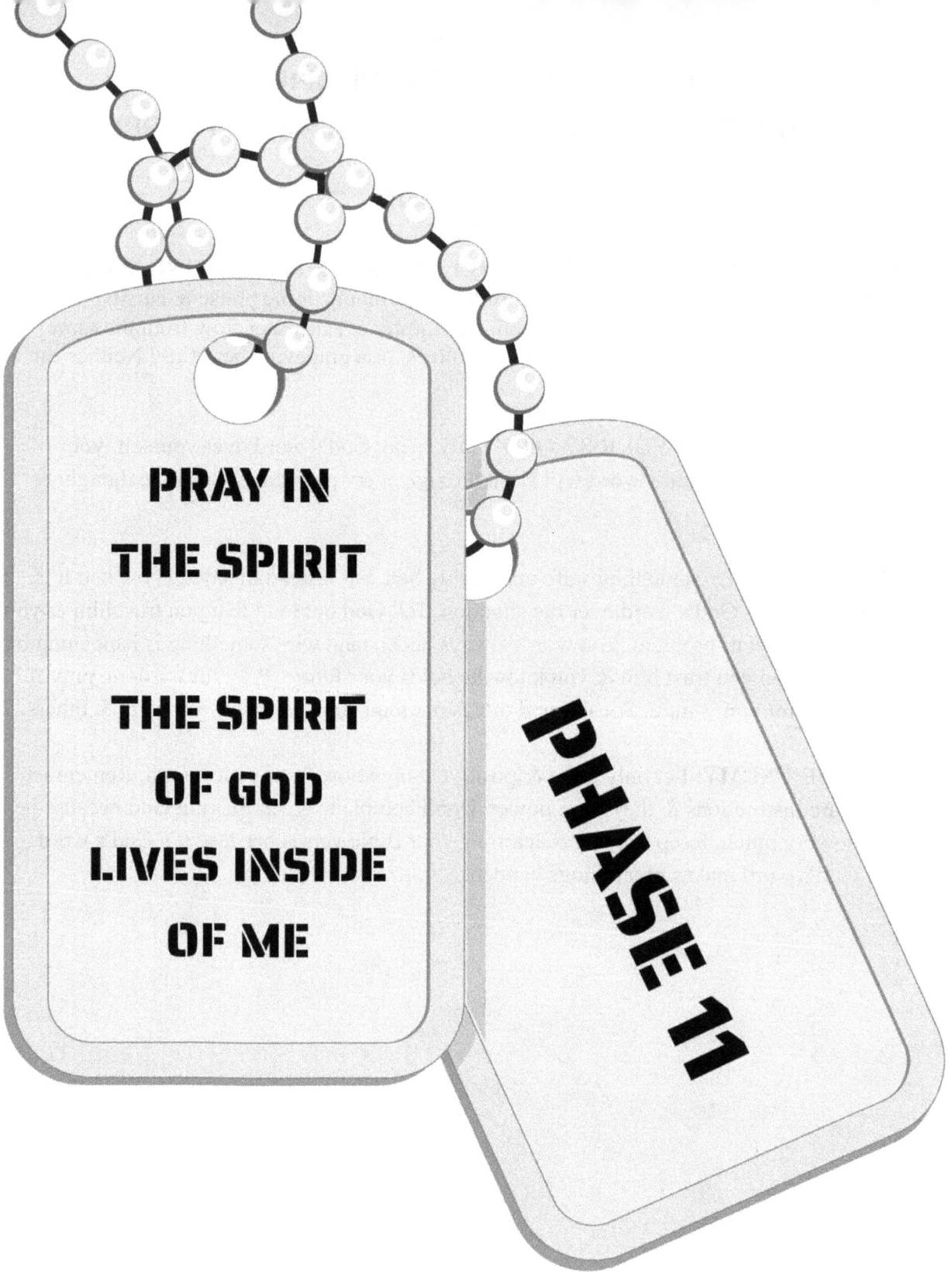

PRAY IN
THE SPIRIT

THE SPIRIT
OF GOD
LIVES INSIDE
OF ME

PHASE 11

PHASE 11: PRAY IN THE SPIRIT
THE SPIRIT OF GOD LIVES INSIDE OF ME

BATTLE PREP

READ ACTS 2

Life can get so hectic at times with situations that have so many different varying factors that it's difficult to know exactly what to do or how to pray. We can make lists of pros & cons & try to analyze things in order to make the best decisions possible for everyone involved but we will never see the whole picture like God does. This is one of the reasons why it is so important to pray in the Spirit with supplication. All of our prayers & communication with God while we move through each day are meaningful & important but we need to make time for God every day where we can get in our quiet place & let the Holy Spirit guide us as we pray. Praying God's word over every situation & asking God to show us what he wants us to see & allowing God's Spirit to minister to us while being patient to listen to God's voice will give us the foresight & wisdom we need to navigate through life.

WEAPONS ASSIGNMENT

John 14:26 But the Advocate, the Holy Spirit, whom the Father will send in my name, will teach you all things & will remind you of everything I have said to you.

COMBAT TRAINING

TELL THE STORY OF THE DAY OF PENTECOST IN ACTS 2

What an amazing time to be alive! Sure, there's a lot of stuff going on in the world that can seem pretty scary for those who don't have Jesus, but if you've accepted Jesus then you never have to worry or fear because God is truly with you. Always! God sent his Spirit to live inside of you. Jesus is always with you! When God sent his Spirit, he wanted everyone to know it & accept Jesus so God's spirit could live in all people. He gave the disciples the ability to speak in other languages so everyone could hear God's message in their language & understand it. It was truly an amazing time, but that time isn't over. God's Spirit is available to all who believe & call on the name of Jesus. God tells us to pray in the Spirit. This means really taking time to pray God's word over all areas of our lives, this is one reason it is important to know our Bible verses. God wants us to make special time for him every day to pray, not only for ourselves but for all God's people everywhere. It's during this special time with God that he will show us things that he wants us to know. If there is ever a time when you feel sad, scared or alone, remember that you are never alone, Jesus is right there with you & he will comfort you & protect you. The Spirit of God lives inside of you!

PHASE 11: PRAY IN THE SPIRIT
THE SPIRIT OF GOD LIVES INSIDE OF ME

RECONNAISSANCE

- Who is God's Spirit for? Everyone.

- Some people thought the disciples were drunk because the way they were acting seemed strange. What are some things that you do or don't do as a Christian that may seem strange to the world? Praying before eating, not watching or listening to certain shows or music that are displeasing to God, not cursing, going to church & reading the Bible, etc.

- When we feel scared, worried or alone, what can we do to help us overcome our fears? Pray, remember God is with us, sing praises to God to help comfort us & take our mind off of our worries & fears, etc.

- When is God's Spirit with us? Always.

THE OBJECTIVE

YOU WILL NEED a UV pen that dries clear, a blacklight & a poster board. Fill the poster board with Bible verses & messages that tell of God's great love for us & how he will never leave us or forsake us.

With the lights on, ask the children to read the messages on the poster. There doesn't seem to be anything there. Ask them to be very still & quiet then turn off the lights & shine the blacklight on to the poster board to reveal & read the messages.

WHAT'S THE POINT? God is with us all the time & there is so much God wants to show us. We couldn't see the messages on the poster but they were there. God is always with us even if we don't see him. A special light was needed to reveal the messages on the poster. For God to reveal messages to us, we have to make special time for him. During this time thank him & praise & ask him to show you what he wants you to see. When we do this, he hears us. He will show you signs & reveal things to you. He might show you a sin that you need to get rid of or he might reveal something that he wants you to do or someone he wants you to help or pray for. It might not happen while you're praying, it might happen throughout your day. God knows how to get through to each & every one of us. He made us & knows us better than we know ourselves & he knows how to get through to each of us, but we have to make time for him & ask him to show us what he wants us to see & teach us what he wants us to know. As we learn God's word & obey it & make special time for God each & every day where we really pour our heart out to him, the Holy Spirit will move in us, he will show us how to pray & exactly what we need to know when we need to know it. God's spirit lives inside of you & God is always with you.

PHASE 11: PRAY IN THE SPIRIT
THE SPIRIT OF GOD LIVES INSIDE OF ME

WEAPONS INSPECTION

John 14:26 But the Advocate, the Holy Spirit, whom the Father will send in my name, will teach you all things & will remind you of everything I have said to you.

PRAY IN THE SPIRIT: Roman soldiers had a secret code that they would use to communicate. These ciphers or secret coded messages would tell them where to go & what to do next. Sometimes, it would warn them about an enemy & tell them how to stay safe. When a soldier was alone on a mission & received these messages, it would always remind him that he was never truly alone & was still a part of a great army. The Holy Spirit speaks to each of us in a special way that is just for us. It's kind of like our own special message from God. When we pray, he will speak to us & let us know he is with us. God will let us know when we shouldn't be doing something, we will get a feeling & know that something is wrong. This is God's Holy Spirit speaking to us. God knows what it takes to get through to each of us because he made us & knows everything about us. The Holy Spirit will comfort us & let us know we are never alone & guide us. When we pray, remember to make time to listen to the Holy Spirit.

PHASE 11: PRAY IN THE SPIRIT
THE SPIRIT OF GOD LIVES INSIDE OF ME

THE MISSION

TO COMPLETE YOUR MISSION YOU WILL NEED THE FOLLOWING WEAPON FROM THE BIBLE: John 14:26 But the Advocate, the Holy Spirit, whom the Father will send in my name, will teach you all things & will remind you of everything I have said to you.

YOUR MISSION: PRAY IN THE SPIRIT! Set special time aside each day to pray & spend with God. It can be at night before bed or in the morning when you wake up or any time that you can devote to God free of interruptions. Find your own special quiet space.

WATCH FOR TRAPS: Rember, God is always with you. If you ever feel scared or alone, know that Jesus is right there with you. If you don't feel like anything is happening when you pray, keep praying & talking to God. Even when we don't feel it, God is still there listening & working things out for us. Our feelings change, but God never changes so ask God to remove any feelings of doubt that you may have & to replace them with only thoughts that are from him.

DEFEAT THE ENEMY: The Holy Spirit is alive inside of you! Keep praying & asking God to show you what he wants you to see & what he wants you to do. God knows exactly how to get through to you. You're learning God's word & obeying it & you're beginning to recognize the voice of God. God is mighty & powerful, but his voice is often a small, quiet voice inside of you. When in doubt about something, seek out what God's word says about it. What you hear from God will always line up with God's word & never contradict it. God is always with you. You are never alone. Keep pouring your heart out to God & he will stir up the Holy Spirit inside of you. You're awesome & you're doing an amazing job!

AMBASSADOR
FOR GOD

I REPRESENT
GOD & WILL
BOLDLY TELL
OTHERS ABOUT
JESUS

PHASE 12

PHASE 12: AMBASSADOR FOR GOD
I REPRESENT GOD & WILL BOLDLY TELL OTHERS ABOUT JESUS

BATTLE PREP

READ MATTHEW 28

Has your world ever been shaken up? You're doing everything you should be but it's so bad that the people around you are scared, worried & panicking? You pray but it seems to get worse? This is probably similar to what Mary was feeling on a grand scale. She was grieving such a great loss, her whole world was changing, nothing would be the same again & all she wanted to do was honor Jesus, her dead loved one who died in such a horrific way, by anointing his body with spices (Mark 16) as was the custom of the time. Instead, there's a violent earthquake, the stone was rolled away from the tomb & the guards, who were the toughest, gnarliest soldiers of their time, trembled in fear until they were frozen in it. However, the angel commanded the women to not be afraid. This is something that is repeated over & over again in God's word, from the old testament to the new. Why? Because faith & fear cannot coexist. If you truly believe God is with you then what or who is there to fear (Romans 8:31)? It is impossible to please God without faith (Hebrews 11:6). God does not give us a spirit of fear (2 Timothy 7). When everything is going right in our world, people don't really pay attention to that. It's easy for us to praise & be full of joy while we are living in an abundance of blessings from such a good God. A blessed life is important for people to see, but when our world turns upside down, that's when they start paying attention. What do we do when our world is shaken up? Do we panic? Do we practice what we preach or do we get so down & afraid that we lose faith? It's not always easy to walk in faith, especially when everyone around you is losing theirs & the enemy is causing confusion. The disciples basically told Mary she was crazy & the Romans were spreading lies that these things never happened. Mary must have felt completely alone, but she never lost her faith or gave in to anger, depression or despair. She did exactly what she was instructed to do. We represent God, the way we respond in every situation matters. We are the body of Christ & how we handle the little stuff & the big things in life makes a difference. If we proclaim to be a Christian then give into fear the moment we experience our own hardships then who is going to want to be a part of that? The world is already full of fear & anxiety. However, when we praise through the storm, press forward with grace & walk in faith until we make it through to brighter days without fear controlling us, that's a true representation of Christ, an Ambassador for God, & it's something that others will want & the world so desperately needs.

WEAPONS ASSIGNMENT

MATTHEW 28:18-20 Then Jesus came to them & said, "All authority of Heaven & on Earth has been given to me. Therefore go & make disciples of all nations, baptizing them in the name of the Father & of the Son & of the Holy Spirit, & teaching them to obey everything I have commanded you. And surely I am with you always, to the very end of the age.

PHASE 12: AMBASSADOR FOR GOD
I REPRESENT GOD & WILL BOLDLY TELL OTHERS ABOUT JESUS

COMBAT TRAINING

TELL THE STORY OF THE RESURRECTION & GREAT COMMISSION IN MATTHEW 28

Mary had a special encounter with Jesus & he told her to go tell the disciples & she did exactly what Jesus told her to do, but even the disciples didn't believe Mary at first. It wasn't until they had their own encounter with Jesus that they believed he was alive & risen from the dead. After Jesus appeared to his disciples, he gave them their mission to go & make disciples out of everyone in the world, so they may be saved, baptized & taught to obey God's word. As Christians, this is our greatest mission in life. Jesus has all the authority in Heaven & Earth & he has given it to us to be ambassadors for God. To be an ambassador means to be a representative. Nations & kingdoms will send ambassadors to speak to kings & other nations of the world & that ambassador will have the authority to speak on behalf of the nation or kingdom that sent them. What they say, how they act & everything they do represents the entire nation he or she is an ambassador for. As Christians, we are ambassadors for all of Heaven, we represent God, & it is our mission to boldly tell others about Jesus. We've had a special encounter with Jesus by hearing God's word, knowing in our hearts that Jesus died for our sins, accepting Jesus as our Lord & receiving salvation & forgiveness from our sins. Because of this, we will live forever in Heaven with Jesus & because God loves us so much, he wants this for everyone. It's our mission to bring the world the message of God's love. As ambassadors of Heaven, our words must always line up with our actions. It's important to always obey God's word & represent God in the way we speak, act & treat others. Our mission is to not only tell others about Jesus but also to teach them to obey God. It's impossible to teach someone how to do something without showing them. The greatest leaders lead by example. By simply living your life in the way God wants you to so others can see how you live & follow your example, you are teaching & leading others. When you tell others about Jesus, don't be discouraged if they don't believe right away. They will have their own special encounter with Jesus & you might not always be there when it happens & that's okay. It's so exciting to be a part of God's kingdom & to be entrusted with such an important mission. You are God's warriors & ambassadors & you're being sent out to recruit others so they too may inherit the Kingdom of Heaven through Jesus.

PHASE 12: AMBASSADOR FOR GOD
I REPRESENT GOD & WILL BOLDLY TELL OTHERS ABOUT JESUS

RECONNAISSANCE

- What was the first thing the angel said to Mary? Do not be afraid! God doesn't want us to be afraid. Fear will keep us from moving & doing what God wants us to do if we let it. The Roman soldiers were so afraid that they couldn't even move but even though Mary & the other Mary were afraid, they went to tell the disciples & they were filled with joy. You might feel afraid to tell people about Jesus, but be brave, you can do it & the more you obey God, the more joy you will have & the easier it will become.

- Not even the disciples believed Mary when she told them that Jesus was alive so don't be discouraged when people don't believe you about Jesus. Mary didn't scream or shout or try to convince them, she simply spoke the truth & allowed Jesus to work out the details in the way he wanted to with each of his disciples. Rember, it's their choice. We are ambassadors & messengers bringing the message of love & salvation not only with our words but by the way we act. Be kind, show love & leave the rest to God.

- The Romans started spreading lies that Jesus wasn't alive & that his disciples stole his body. There are still lies being told to this day. What are some lies that the world believes? False religions, false gods, Jesus isn't the son of God, there is no such thing as God, there isn't a Heaven or a hell, God didn't create the world, etc. There are so many lies people have been told. Some people have been told these lies by their parents since they were very young. They tell these lies because they have been told to them, they believe them & don't think they are wrong. Many people think these lies are good & the truth is bad, but it doesn't mean these people are bad, it means they are lost. God loves them & sent Jesus to save them. Remember, you're on a mission to rescue the lost by sharing the message of God's great love & salvation through Jesus, the one & only way to Heaven.

- When the disciples gathered together at the mountain where Jesus told them to go, it was there Jesus appeared to them & told them that he had all authority in Heaven & all of the Earth & he gave this authority to his disciples, including each of you, to carry out the mission of making disciples out of all nations by sharing the message of God's love & salvation through Jesus with everyone. We've been given the authority to represent God & to speak for God by telling others about Jesus & to teach for God by showing others how to obey God through love & kindness & our own obedience to God.

PHASE 12: AMBASSADOR FOR GOD
I REPRESENT GOD & WILL BOLDLY TELL OTHERS ABOUT JESUS

THE OBJECTIVE

YOU WILL NEED a police officer dressed in uniform. If you don't have one in your church or are unable to find a volunteer, you can use a picture.

When an officer of the law is uniform, everyone knows who they are working for & who they represent. A police officer represents his entire city. In fact, they are sworn to uphold & protect the law even when they are off duty & out of uniform. They are held to a higher standard. Why? Because of who & what they represent. They represent their entire city & the governing forces of the city such as the courts, the judges & the mayor. They are there to serve & protect the people. What would you think if you saw a police officer stealing from the store or robbing a bank? Would you feel safe? Would you believe in the law? Seeing even one police officer act like this would definitely cause confusion in most people's minds. What if you were searching for a place to live & you saw several police officers in one city going around town littering, stealing from stores, breaking the laws & being unkind to the people, would you want to live in that city? Nobody would want to live there.

WHAT'S THE POINT? We represent God. Once we become a Christian, it is like wearing a uniform 24/7. The world looks at us & determines how God is by the way we act & how we treat them. If we're not kind to one another or if we're disobedient to God, then this causes confusion & causes people to not trust in the true message of God's love & salvation. Instead, they seek out other religions & believe lies. Why? Because if the ones who claim to represent God break his laws, then it's hard to learn the truth. Sadly, this happens a lot in the world today. God is still the same loving God no matter what we do or how we act but the way people get to know God is by how we treat each other & by the life we live. If we claim to be a Christian & represent God then it's our duty to uphold God's law & live in a way that shows the world who God really is. It's a huge responsibility but it is also a great honor to be an ambassador for God on the most important mission in the world to boldly share the message of God's love & salvation through Jesus. It's a life saving mission! You are brave & courageous & you are never alone. Jesus is with you always. God's Holy Spirit lives inside you. You put on the whole armor of God every day & you have all of Heaven backing you so you can accomplish everything God created you to do!

PHASE 12: AMBASSADOR FOR GOD
I REPRESENT GOD & WILL BOLDLY TELL OTHERS ABOUT JESUS

WEAPONS INSPECTION

MATTHEW 28:18-20 Then Jesus came to them & said, "All authority of Heaven & on Earth has been given to me. Therefore go & make disciples of all nations, baptizing them in the name of the Father & of the Son & of the Holy Spirit, & teaching them to obey everything I have commanded you. And surely I am with you always, to the very end of the age.

AMBASSADOR FOR GOD: Ancient Rome had ambassadors called legati, just like we have ambassadors today for countries & kingdoms. Ambassadors represent their country & have the authority to speak on behalf of kings, presidents & leaders. Ambassadors are sent to other countries to deliver important messages & sometimes their job can be a little scary & dangerous because they don't know how others will react to the message. However, ambassadors also receive many benefits, they have their entire country backing them, they are paid very well & when they retire, they will never have to worry about money again. When you deliver the message of God's love & salvation to others, it might be a little scary at first but it will get easier every time you do it. There's no greater message in the world than the message of God's great love & salvation through Jesus, & even though ambassadors on Earth are well taken care of, it's nothing compared to the benefits you receive as an ambassador for God. God promises to supply all your needs according to his riches & glory. You have all of Heaven backing you. You have the Holy Spirit with you at all times & a heavenly army that will go to war on your behalf. You have a loving & mighty God who is always guiding your every step & as far as retirement goes, when your life on Earth is done, you will inherit the Kingdom of Heaven & live forever with Jesus in a place that he has prepared for you.

PHASE 12: AMBASSADOR FOR GOD
I REPRESENT GOD & WILL BOLDLY TELL OTHERS ABOUT JESUS

THE MISSION

TO COMPLETE YOUR MISSION YOU WILL NEED THE FOLLOWING WEAPON FROM THE BIBLE: MATTHEW 28:18-20 Then Jesus came to them & said, "All authority of Heaven & on Earth has been given to me. Therefore go & make disciples of all nations, baptizing them in the name of the Father & of the Son & of the Holy Spirit, & teaching them to obey everything I have commanded you. And surely I am with you always, to the very end of the age.

YOUR MISSION: REPRESENT GOD & BE HIS AMBASSADOR! Boldly tell others about Jesus! You're on a mission to save the lost & bring the message of God's love & salvation through Jesus to as many people as you can. God chose you for this special assignment. You can do it!

WATCH FOR TRAPS: Don't be afraid. The Holy Spirit is always with you, you have all of Heaven backing you. The enemy is busy spreading lies & trying to confuse people; Satan doesn't want people to know Jesus is the son of God & the only way to Heaven. Don't engage in arguments, but instead teach them about God's great love through kindness & obedience to God. Never forget that you represent God as his ambassador.

DEFEAT THE ENEMY: Don't be afraid. Remember, Jesus is always with you. The Holy Spirit lives inside of you. Take a stand against the enemy as an ambassador for God & boldly tell others about Jesus! Put on the full armor of God every single day & never take it off! You are now on a lifelong assignment to win the lost for Jesus. YOU'RE AN AMBASSADOR FOR GOD!

ARMOR OF GOD

- **BELT OF TRUTH:** Jesus is my belt of truth. I will always put Jesus first & make him the center of my world!
- **BREASTPLATE OF RIGHTEOUSNESS:** I will make my feelings & thoughts obey God.
- **SANDALS OF PEACE:** Obeying God prepares me for anything & prevents me from falling into temptation.
- **SHIELD OF FAITH:** I know God will never fail me. God will always keep his promises & do what he said he will do.
- **HELMET OF SALVATION:** I will keep my mind renewed & protected by filling it with God's word.
- **SWORD OF THE SPIRIT:** The Bible is my sword & I will learn it, obey it & speak it!